WOODWORKING
PROJECTS IV

49 Easy-to-Make Projects

A Shopsmith®/Rodale Press Publication

Shopsmith®, Inc.
3931 Image Drive
Dayton, Ohio 45414

Rodale Press, Inc.
33 East Minor Street
Emmaus, Pennsylvania 18098

Preface

This book contains forty-nine woodworking project plans from back issues of HANDS ON, The Home Workshop Magazine published by Shopsmith, Inc., Pete Prlain's *How-to with Wood,* and Simpson's *Book of Wood/ Could* projects.

These easy-to-make projects are sure to provide any woodworker, from beginner to expert, with hours of fun and enjoyment in the shop. Many of the projects are ideal gifts for family or friends, and they are suitable for most any occasion—Christmas, birthdays, weddings.

Note that some of the projects were designed to be made using a Shopsmith router arm; these are designated by the symbol ▢ . Feel free to revise the procedures as needed to do the projects with a conventional router setup. Special woodworking techniques have been referred to in *Power Tool Woodworking for Everyone* by R. J. DeCristoforo, Reston Publishing Company.

Our thanks go out to the many readers who have contributed their project ideas over the years. Their ideas continue to provide inspiration and enjoyment for their fellow woodworkers.

A final note: As with any woodworking endeavor, always keep safety your top priority when undertaking these projects. Plan your work carefully before you begin, and always use the recommended tools and procedures. Be sure to study every project plan thoroughly, including the diagrams and list of materials, before making any cuts.

Library of Congress Cataloging-in-Publication Data
Woodworking projects.

Includes indexes.
Contents: (1) 60 easy-to-make projects from Hands on magazine—(etc.)—3. 46 easy-to-make projects—4. 49 easy-to-make projects.
1. Woodwork.   I. Shopsmith, Inc.   II. Hands on! (Dayton, Ohio).
TT180.W66   1986   684'.08   85-29792
ISBN 0-87857-618-5 (vol. 1 hardcover)
ISBN 0-87857-615-0 (vol. 1 paperback)

ISBN 0-87857-784-X (hardcover)
ISBN 0-87857-780-7 (paperback)

Printed in the United States of America on recycled paper containing a high percentage of de-inked fiber.

Rodale Press Edition

1988
10 9 8 7 6 5 4 3 2 1 hardcover
10 9 8 7 6 5 4 3 2 1 paperback

Publisher: Shopsmith®, Inc/Rodale Press, Inc.
Text Preparation: Scharff Associates, Ltd.
Cover Photography: Mitchell T. Mandel

Contents

Odds and Ends

The projects in this section are best summed up in one word: unique. There's one for every taste, and all are guaranteed to add color and charm to any room in your home.

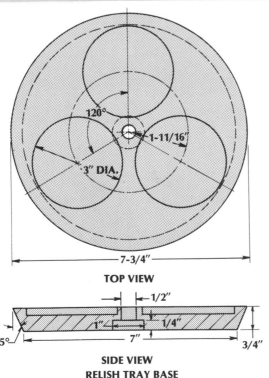

TOP VIEW

120°

1-11/16"

3" DIA.

7-3/4"

15°

1/2"

1"

1/4"

7"

3/4"

SIDE VIEW
RELISH TRAY BASE

This relish tray makes a perfect gift, especially when it's filled with homemade relishes. It can also be used as a breakfast jam set or as a cocktail set for various types of nuts. The first step is to purchase three double old-fashioned glasses; the rest of the project depends on the measurements of the glasses you use. This example uses clear, heavy-bottomed glasses measuring 2-3/4" high, with a 2-3/4" diameter at the bottom and a 3-3/16" diameter at the top.

All of the wood pieces can be made from a single square foot of nominal 1-inch stock of your choice. Lay out the pieces to the dimensions of the glasses, leaving a 1/4" overlap (1/8" on each side) over the outside diameter of the glasses for the covers. The procedure is as follows:

1. Cut out the three covers (B) on a bandsaw or jigsaw. If you do not have 1-5/8"-thick stock, you might want to cut out three 3/4" × 3/4" × 1" pieces to be glued to the top of the covers to make the knobs.

2. Make a template as a guide to produce the three circular recesses in the base.

3. Rout the recesses 1/4" deep. You might want to get that depth in two or three passes.

4. Remove the base from the template, then cut it out with a bandsaw. For a fancy edge, mount the base on a faceplate and turn to the desired design.

5. Drill a 1"-diameter counterbore 1/4" deep in the center of the bottom of the base. Finish drilling with a 1/2" bit, being careful not to break the surface around the top of the hole.

6. Glue the knob pieces that were cut in step 1 to the covers. Clamp and allow the pieces to set for 24 hours before turning. To turn the covers, mount each one directly to a screw center. Turn the main diameter of the glass plus an extra 1/4", then turn to fit the inside di-

LIST OF MATERIALS

(finished dimensions in inches)

A	Base	7-3/4 dia. × 3/4
B	Covers (3)	3-1/4 dia. × 1-5/8
C	Handle shaft	5/8 dia. × 6-1/4
D	Handle	5/8 dia. × 3
	Double old-fashioned glasses (3)	
	Roundhead wood screw	
	Flat washer	
	Felt	
	Wood glue	

ameter of the glass. Shape the tops of the covers to the desired design.
7. Drill a 1/2"-diameter hole 1/2" deep in the center of the handle stock. Turn the handle and handle shaft to the desired design, leaving a 1/2" shank about 1/2" long on the top and bottom of the handle shaft.
8. Glue the handle to the handle shaft. Then attach the shaft to the base with a flat washer and screw.
9. Finish with a good polyurethane satin finish. When dry, glue a circular piece of felt to the bottom of the tray for protection, but remember to make a hole in the center of the felt so the washer and screw are not covered.

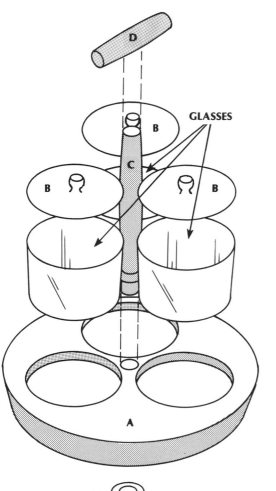

GLASSES

RELISH TRAY ASSEMBLY

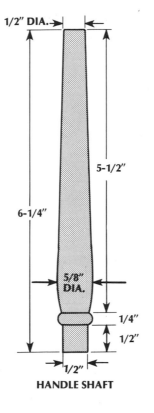

HANDLE SHAFT

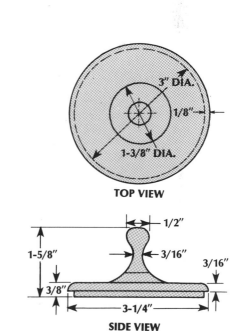

TOP VIEW

SIDE VIEW
RELISH CONTAINER COVER

5/8" DIA.

END VIEW

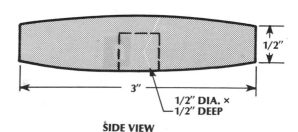

1/2" DIA. ×
1/2" DEEP

SIDE VIEW

HANDLE

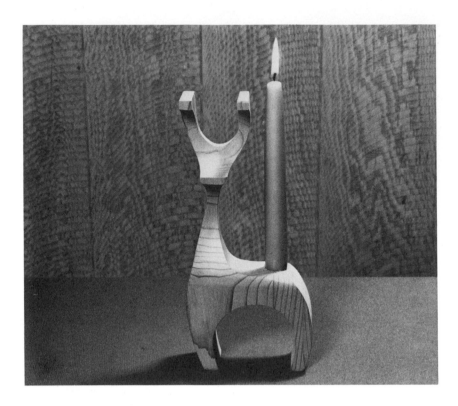

LIST OF MATERIALS

(finished dimensions in inches)

Body	1-3/4 × 5 × 10-1/2
24-ga. sheet metal	1-3/4 × 8-1/4 (bookends only)
Flathead wood screws	#10 × 3/4 (bookends only)
Candle	3/4 dia. × 12 (candleholder only)

Bookends and candleholders are useful items to have around the house, and this design can be used as both! Compound cuts on a bandsaw are used to make the deer shape, the same technique used to make three-dimensional wooden shapes such as cabriole legs and chess pieces. The list of materials gives the amount of materials needed to make one set of bookends and one candleholder.

1. Make a cardboard or Masonite template of the front and side deer patterns. Trace the patterns on 4"-thick × 6"-wide stock; two deer can be cut from every 11" length of stock.

2. The compound cutting technique is as follows: Cut the side contour first, then tape the pieces back together, turn the workpiece 90°, and cut the front contour.

3. Use a drum sander and belt sander to reach all of the deer's curved surfaces.

4. If making bookends, cut 24-gauge sheet metal into 1-3/4" × 8" pieces. Attach them to the feet of the deer with #10 × 3/4" flathead wood screws through the feet.

5. If making candleholders, drill a 3/4"-diameter hole 3/4" deep into the back of the deer.

6. Finish as desired.

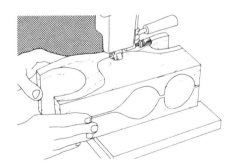

Cut the side contour on a bandsaw.

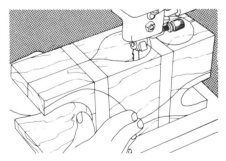

Cut the front contour on a bandsaw.

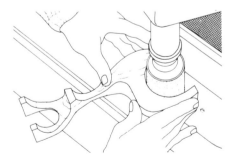

Sand the deer with a drum sander.

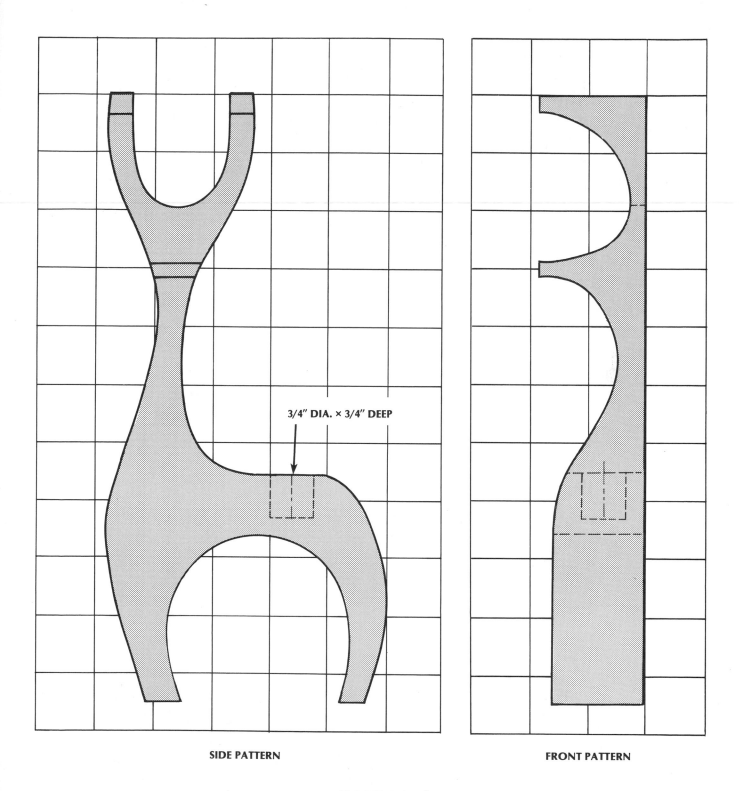

3/4" DIA. × 3/4" DEEP

SIDE PATTERN

FRONT PATTERN

ONE SQUARE = 1"

9

WINE SERVER

Offer wine to your guests with this easy-to-make server and you're sure to be a hit, especially if you're the creator of both the server and the wine.

1. Cut two pieces of stock—one 9-1/4" square and the other 10-1/4" square. Sand the surfaces to remove all mill marks.

2. Mark the centers of the eight holes in the top ring (A), as well as the outside circular contour and the inside circle.

3. Attach the top ring stock to the base stock (B) with a #18 × 1" brad in each corner so the centers line up. Drill four 1/2"-diameter holes through both pieces to accommodate the columns (C).

4. Disassemble the two pieces, then drill four 3/4"-diameter holes in the top ring for the glasses.

5. Using a jigsaw or saber saw, cut the inside and outside circles in the top ring. Be careful to stay 1/32" to 1/16" on the scrap side of the lines. Then sand the edges to the lines using drum and disc sanders.

6. Rout the edge of the top ring to the desired shape. The drawing shows a 3/8" bead, but be as creative as you want.

7. Repeat steps 5 and 6 on the base.

8. Cut the 9/16"-wide slots in the top ring to allow the glasses to slide into the holes drilled in step 4. The server is now ready to assemble.

9. Apply glue to the holes in the base, and insert the columns flush with the bottom. Do the same with the top ring, making sure to remove excess glue with a damp rag.

10. When the glue has dried, it might be necessary to touch up the top and bottom of the server where the columns protrude. This can be done with a piece of sandpaper and a sanding block. Finish sand with 180-grit paper.

11. Finish as desired.

12. Glue a cork base to the bottom of the server to complete the project.

LIST OF MATERIALS

(finished dimensions in inches)

A	Top ring	3/4 × 9 dia.
B	Base	3/4 × 10 dia.
C	Columns (4)	1/2 dia. × 7 dowels
	Cork	1/16 × 4-3/4 dia.
	Brads	#18 × 1
	Wood glue	

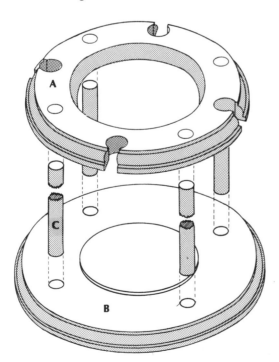

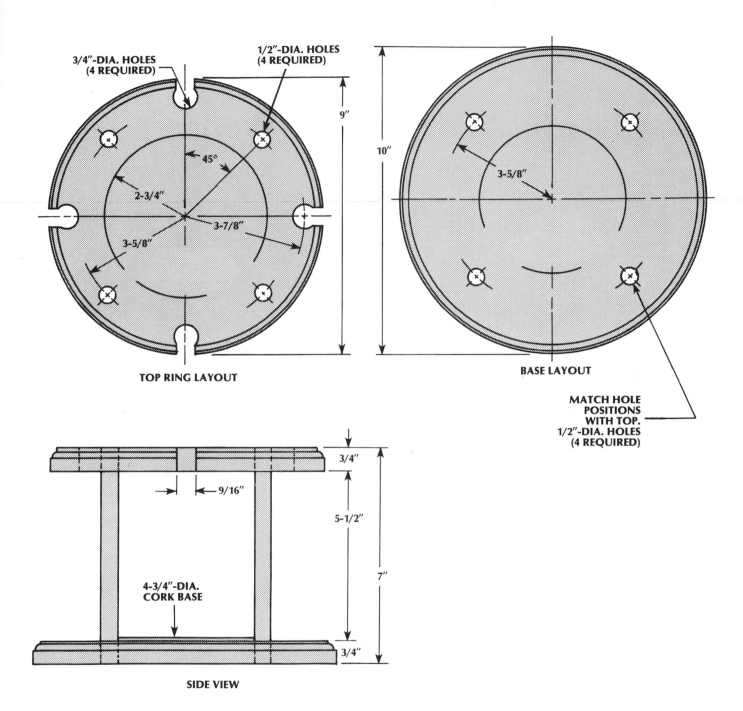

3/4"-DIA. HOLES (4 REQUIRED)

1/2"-DIA. HOLES (4 REQUIRED)

45°

2-3/4"

3-7/8"

3-5/8"

9"

TOP RING LAYOUT

10"

3-5/8"

BASE LAYOUT

MATCH HOLE POSITIONS WITH TOP. 1/2"-DIA. HOLES (4 REQUIRED)

3/4"

9/16"

5-1/2"

7"

4-3/4"-DIA. CORK BASE

3/4"

SIDE VIEW

Around picture frame is an interesting change from the standard rectangular type. With the help of a specially made fixture and the technique of pin routing, you can make this frame in no time at all.

MAKING THE FIXTURE

1. Transfer the circle pattern provided to a piece of 1/2" plywood.
2. Use a saber saw, bandsaw, or jigsaw to cut out a circle with the diameter "A."
3. Drill two 3/16"-diameter screw holes at the points indicated. Screw the plywood cutout to a piece of laminated countertop. If possible, use a waste piece such as a sink cutout.
4. Using a 3/8" straight flute, carbide tip router bit, cut a 3/8"-deep groove in the laminate side of the fixture as shown. After the groove has been cut, remove the plywood pattern from the fixture.
5. Again using a saber saw, bandsaw, or jigsaw, cut out a circle with the diameter "B."
6. Reattach the plywood pattern on the bottom of the fixture, mak-

ing sure it is in the exact location as when you cut the first groove. Now cut the 3/8" groove for circle B, then remove the pattern.
7. Repeat steps 5 and 6 to cut circle C and its groove.
NOTE: Groove A cuts the outside dimension of the frame and can also be followed when cutting decorative outside edges. Groove B is used for the decorative design in the frame. Groove C provides the "daylight" opening for the picture.
8. Drill two 3/16"-diameter screw holes through the fixture at the point where the plywood pattern was attached. Then drill two more holes of the same size at opposite ends of the fixture, midpoint between grooves A and B.
9. Flip the fixture over and countersink the screw holes in the laminate side so the heads of #8 screws

will be completely recessed when inserted. The fixture is now complete.

MAKING THE FRAME

1. Attach the workpiece to the particleboard side of the fixture with #8 × 1" wood screws. Insert the screws in the countersunk holes drilled previously in steps 8 and 9. The heads of the screws must lie flush with or below the surface of the laminate.
2. Lay the fixture on the router table, with the outside edge of the fixture against the 3/8" table pin. With the router turned off, lower the 3/8" straight bit until it barely touches the particleboard surface. Set the depth-of-cut using the depth-stop rod.
3. With the workpiece still attached, flip the fixture over and set it on the pin to cut the outside edge of the frame (line A). When cutting the outside edge, make no less than three separate cuts.
4. Repeat steps 2 and 3 to cut the "daylight" opening (line C).
5. To make the decorative cut in the frame, set the fixture over groove B and readjust the depth-of-cut to produce the desired design. Do not cut too deeply or you will hit one of the attachment screws.
6. Use a rounding over bit to round the edges of the frame at lines C and A.
7. When all cuts have been made, remove the frame from the fixture. With a 3/4" straight bit centered over the 3/8" pin, guide the inside edge of the daylight opening against the pin. Lower the bit to make the 1/4"-deep rabbet needed for inserting the picture and glass.
8. To complete the frame, finish as desired.

LIST OF MATERIALS

(finished dimensions in inches)

Workpiece	3/4 × 12 × 12
Wood screws	#8 × 1
1/2" plywood	
Laminated countertop	

NOTE: BY MAKING YOUR FIXTURE AND WORKPIECE LARGE ENOUGH AND ALIGNING THE WORKPIECE PERFECTLY ON THE FIXTURE, YOU CAN MAKE A SQUARE FRAME WITH A ROUND CUTOUT AT THE SAME TIME YOU ARE MAKING YOUR ROUND FRAME.

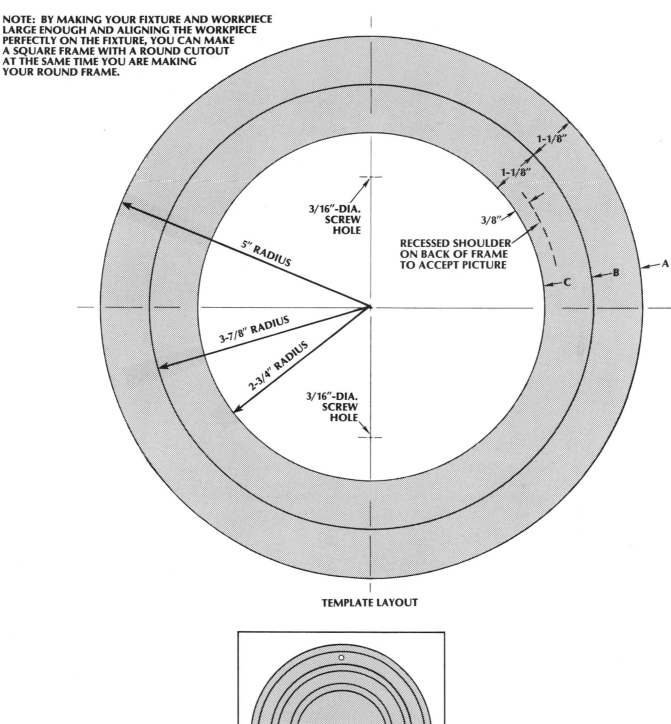

1-1/8″

1-1/8″

3/16″-DIA. SCREW HOLE

3/8″

RECESSED SHOULDER ON BACK OF FRAME TO ACCEPT PICTURE

5″ RADIUS

3-7/8″ RADIUS

2-3/4″ RADIUS

3/16″-DIA. SCREW HOLE

A

B

C

TEMPLATE LAYOUT

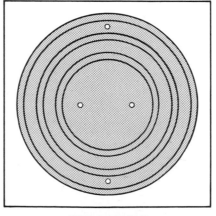

FIXTURE DETAIL

SERVING TRAY

LIST OF MATERIALS

(finished dimensions in inches)

A	Tray	3/4 × 13 × 15
B	Tray handles (2)	3/4 × 3 × 13
C	Caddy handle	3/8 × 3 × 5
D	Caddy bottom	3/8 × 3 × 12
E	Caddy sides (2)	3/8 × 3 × 13
F	Caddy ends (2)	3/8 × 2-3/4 × 3
	Tiles (2)	1/4 × 6 × 6
	Decorative hinges (2)	
	Brads	
	Wood glue	

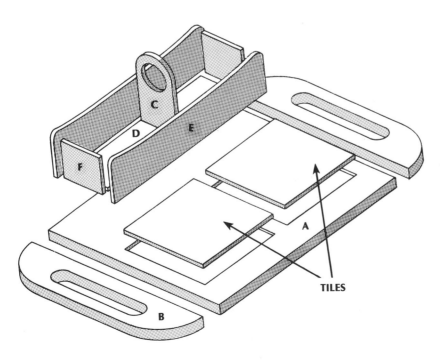

TILES

This handy serving tray has two inlaid tiles to prevent hot dishes from scorching the wood. The handles fold up for easy carrying, then fold down flat on the table while you serve. As an added feature, the tiles provide a scrubbable surface on which you can arrange hors d'oeuvres.

1. An 11-1/4 × 31" board is enough for the 3/4" stock; an 11-1/4" × 20" board is sufficient 3/8" stock to make the caddy. Begin by cutting 15" off the 3/4" board and set it aside.

2. From the remaining 3/4" stock, rip two 3" pieces and one 2-3/4" piece. Glue the 2-3/4" piece to the 15" piece cut in step 1 to form the tray (A).

3. Attach the stock for the two tray handles (B) face to face with nails through the handle area. Cut out the outside of the handles on a jigsaw, then cut the inside contours to the dimensions given.

4. Smooth the glue joint on the tray, then cut the recesses for the tiles and hinges using a router and a hand chisel to square the corners.

5. Depending on personal preference, the 3/8" caddy stock can be substituted with plywood. If using solid lumber and you do not have access to a surfacer, the stock must be cut to the proper thickness on a bandsaw or table saw. Sand or plane the machined surface smooth.

6. Cut out the caddy handle (C), bottom (D), sides (E), and ends (F) to size. Attach the sides together and cut their contours, as was done with the tray handles in step 3.

7. Cut out the 1-1/2"-diameter hole in the caddy handle.

8. Sand all sawed pieces. You are now ready to assemble the serving tray.

9. Assembly is done with brads and wood glue. Begin with the caddy, first attaching the ends to the bottom, then the handle to the bottom. Finally, add the sides. Be sure all brad heads are set below the surface and the holes filled with putty.

10. Finish all pieces before further assembly. A dark cherry, mahogany, or walnut stain is recommended, followed by a good heat-resistant finish such as polyurethane. Be careful not to get any stain or finish in the tile recesses.

11. Attach the tray handles to the tray using decorative hinges.

12. Glue the tiles in the recesses with tile or ceramic cement.

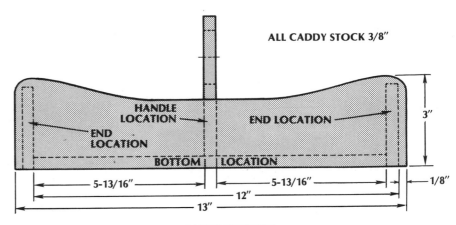

ALL CADDY STOCK 3/8"

CADDY SIDE VIEW

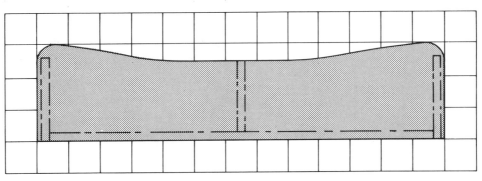

ONE SQUARE = 1"   **CADDY SIDE TEMPLATE**

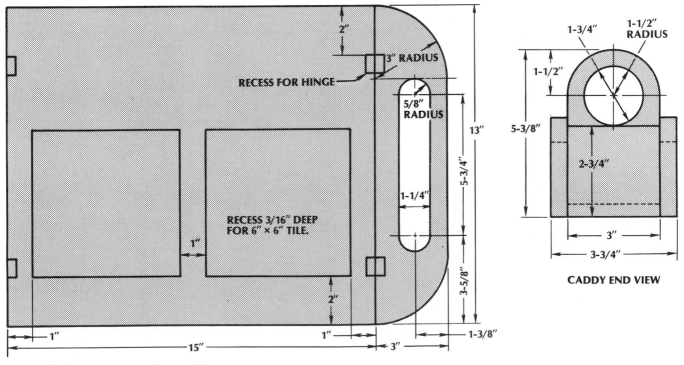

TRAY TOP VIEW

CADDY END VIEW

CANDLE SCONCE

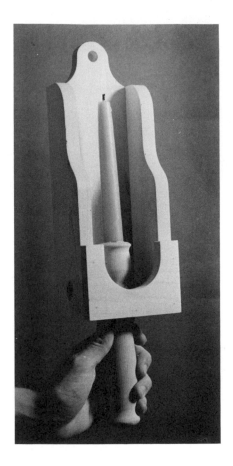

In colonial times, the candle sconce was used much like our modern-day flashlight. This sconce, copied from a traditional Shaker design, can be mounted on a wall or carried by its handle. If desired, plywood can be substituted for the 3/8" pine that was used in this example.

1. Cut all of the pieces to rough size, leaving an extra 1/8" on the length of the back (A) and the sides (B). Sand all face surfaces before cutting the contours using the patterns provided.

2. Drill a 3/8"-diameter hole in the back, and a 1/4"-diameter hole in the bottom (D), as shown. Then finish sand all flat surfaces and edges.

3. Turn the handle (E) and base (F) from a single piece of 7" long stock. Leave about 3/8" between the handle and base, and about 1" at the headstock end for the rounded bottom of the handle.

4. After turning, sand completely. Use the parting tool to almost separate the base from the handle at the bottom edge of the base. Do this at a slow RPM. Remove from the lathe and cut apart using a bandsaw or handsaw.

5. Drill a 1/4"-diameter hole in the center of the bottom of the base to accommodate a dowel. Drill a 3/4"-diameter hole 3/4" to 1" deep in the top of the base to fit the candle. Clamp the base to the drill press when drilling; do not hand hold.

6. If necessary, touch up the ends of the base and handle on a disc sander.

7. Begin assembly by coating the bottom inside edge of the back with glue and attaching the bottom. Then coat the edges of the back with glue, one at a time, and secure the sides to the back and bottom with #18 × 1" brads.

8. Coat the lower inside edge of the front (C) with glue and secure it to the sides and bottom with brads.

9. To attach the handle and base, apply glue to all three holes, then slip the 1/4"-diameter dowel through the bottom and into the base. Attach the handle and secure with a clamp.

NOTE: Be sure to scrub off excess glue immediately with a damp rag. Any glue left behind will ruin the finished sconce.

10. Set all brads below the surface, and fill with wood putty.

11. Finish sand, then apply finish as desired.

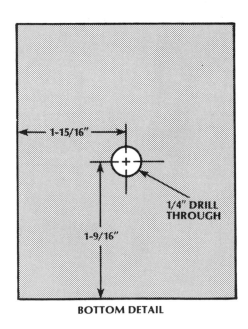

1-15/16"

1-9/16"

1/4" DRILL THROUGH

BOTTOM DETAIL

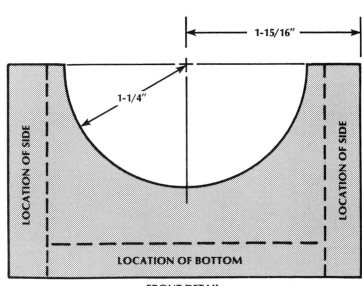

1-15/16"

1-1/4"

LOCATION OF SIDE

LOCATION OF SIDE

LOCATION OF BOTTOM

FRONT DETAIL

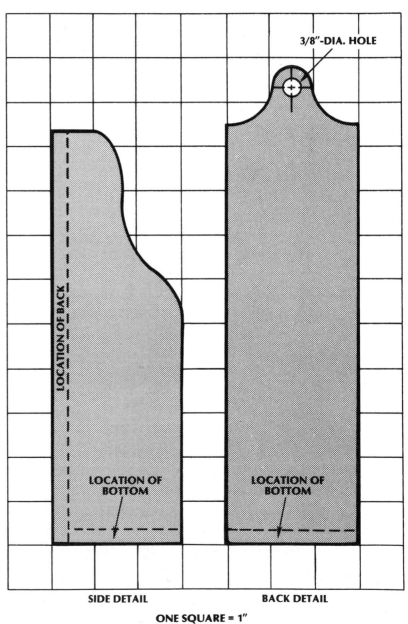

LIST OF MATERIALS

(finished dimensions in inches)

A	Back	3/8 × 3-1/8 × 10-3/4
B	Sides (2)	3/8 × 3 × 9-3/8
C	Front	3/8 × 3-7/8 × 2-1/4
D	Bottom	3/8 × 2-5/8 × 3-1/8
E	Handle	1-1/8 dia. × 3-3/4
F	Base	1-1/8 dia. × 2
	Dowel	1/4 dia. × 1-3/8
	Brads	#18 × 1
	Wood putty	
	Wood glue	

DOWEL

3/4″ DIA. × 3/4″ DEEP

BASE
1-1/8″ DIA. × 2″
(MAKE ONE)

2″

1/4 DIA. ×
1/2″ DEEP

3-3/4″

HANDLE
1-1/8″ DIA. ×
3-3/4″

3/8″-DIA. HOLE

LOCATION OF BACK

LOCATION OF
BOTTOM

LOCATION OF
BOTTOM

SIDE DETAIL

BACK DETAIL

ONE SQUARE = 1″

Everyone loves the intricate shapes and natural beauty of wooden jewelry. By working with different types of wood and various thicknesses of stock, you can make designs as beautiful as the finest stones. Experiment all you want—you're limited only by your imagination.

An important step in making wooden jewelry is laminating the wood to create different designs. There are two ways of laminating stock, depending on the design. One way is to glue-up thin layers of stock or veneer; the second involves cutting slots in a block of wood and then gluing contrasting stock or veneer in the slots. When laminating, always allow the glue to dry to the manufacturer's recommendations before machining.

SPIRAL DESIGN

The spiral design is made by following a special laminating procedure.

1. Start with any square block; a good size is 3/16" × 1-1/2" × 1-1/2". Set your bandsaw table at an angle between 4° and 10° so that the blade will cut from one corner to the opposite corner.

2. Using a 1/16" or other thin-gauge blade with a cut equal in width to the thickness of your veneer, cut a slot one-third of the way into each of the four sides of the block.

3. Mark the center in the top and bottom of the block, then drill a 3/8"-diameter hole halfway through it.

4. Using a plug cutter, cut out a 3/8"-diameter plug from contrasting stock and glue it in the hole to provide a decorative center dot. Leave the plug long as shown and use it to hold the stock.

5. Cut strips from the same contrasting stock and glue them into the slots in the block. Clamp at least two of the sides with spring clamps or spring-type clothespins. Allow at least four hours for the glue to dry.

6. Using a compass, draw a circle on the bottom of the block. Cut out the shape with a bandsaw.

7. Insert the dowel into the chuck of a hand drill. While the dowel rotates, hold the circular piece against a disc sander rotating in the opposite direction. Use a coarse disc to sand the piece to a dome-shaped contour, then sand it smooth with a fine disc.

8. Remove the piece from the drill chuck, cut off the dowel, then sand the back of the piece smooth. Finish with an oil finish or high-gloss polyurethane.

9. Using epoxy cement, glue on the appropriate hardware to make an earring, pendant, cuff link, or tie clasp. The hardware is available at most major craft stores.

HERRINGBONE DESIGN

A herringbone design is made in the following manner:

1. Cut out small strips from two contrasting pieces of wood.

2. Glue the strips face-to-face, alternating colors, and clamp

3. After allowing the glue to dry, cut the glued-up block at a 10° to 15° angle into strips of alternate color.

4. Turn every other strip end for end, glue them face-to-face again, and allow to dry.

5. Cut off thin strips from the end of the block to complete the herringbone design. It can be glued to a backup block for turning.

POLYGONAL CENTER DESIGN

To make a polygonal center design, follow this procedure:

1. Cut a block of wood to any polygonal shape.

2. Glue several contrasting wood pieces around alternate sides. True-up the sides, then glue contrasting pieces to the remaining sides.

3. Repeat with different kinds of woods and different thicknesses of stock for varying effect.

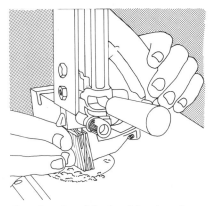

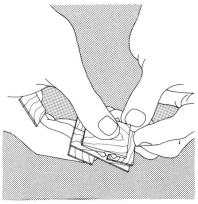

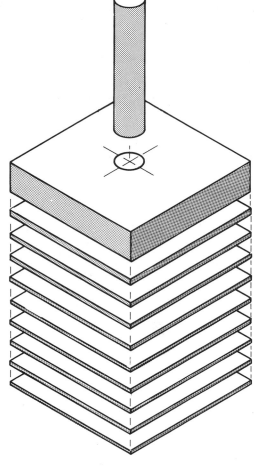

Cut slots in a block with a bandsaw set between 4° and 10°.

Glue strips into the slots.

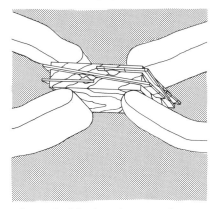

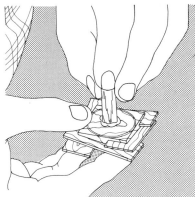

Clamp the block with spring clamps.

Glue dowel onto block for turning.

CONSTRUCTION DETAIL

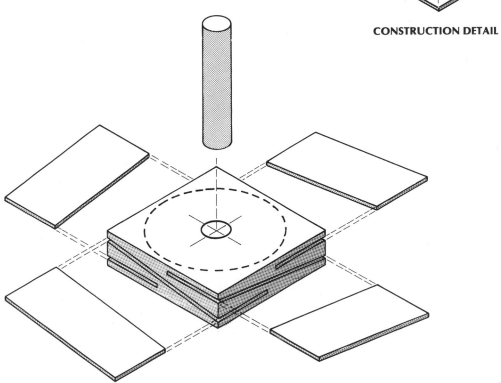

Nothing illuminates a porch or patio better than an attractive coach lantern. If desired, colored plastic can be mounted inside the lantern to soften the lighting effect. Use a special fixture and the technique of pin routing if desired, or omit the router and make it a "regular" woodworking project. Note that the fixture is designed to cut the top, bottom, and side pieces of the lantern. The recommended wood for this project is 3/4" pine.

1. Transfer the pattern for the sides (A) and the pattern for the top (B) and bottom (C) to a piece of 1/2" plywood.

2. Cut out the patterns, then screw them to the particleboard side of a piece of plastic-laminated particleboard. Using a 3/8" straight bit, cut 3/8"-deep grooves in the laminate side of the fixture. When all of the patterns have been cut, remove the plywood pattern from the fixture.

3. Cut two pieces of wood into 7-3/4" × 12" lengths, and two

pieces into 7-3/4" × 20-1/4" lengths. Each long piece will make one side and the top or bottom; each short piece will make one side.

4. Align the 3/8" bit and the 3/8" table pin perfectly, and set the depth-stop rod so the bit barely cuts through the workpiece when mounted in the fixture.

5. Clamp the workpiece into the fixture, turn the fixture over, and guide the pin through all the grooves. Make at least three cuts in each area to avoid forcing the bit through the workpiece too rapidly.

6. Change to a chamfering bit to "dress" the edges of the cutout areas. If a decorative touch is not desired, simply sand the edges.

7. Divide the two long pieces to form one side and the top or bottom. Then cut the remaining scrap off the top/bottom piece, making it exactly 7-3/4" square. The lantern is now ready to assemble.

8. Cut a 3/4"-wide × 3/8"-deep rabbet on the 12" side of two of the side pieces. Then remove 3/8" from each side of the remaining two 7-3/4"-wide side pieces; these narrower side pieces will fit into the rabbeted areas on the other two pieces that were just cut.

NOTE: For a more professional-looking appearance, the lantern can be assembled using 45° mi-

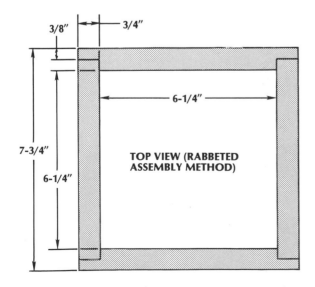

TOP VIEW (RABBETED ASSEMBLY METHOD)

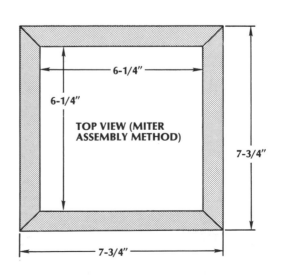

TOP VIEW (MITER ASSEMBLY METHOD)

LIST OF MATERIALS

(finished dimensions in inches)

A	Sides (4)	3/4 × 7-3/4 × 12
B	Top	3/4 × 7-3/4 × 7-3/4
C	Bottom	3/4 × 7-3/4 × 7-3/4
	Light socket	
	Hook and chain	
	2d finishing nails	
	Wood glue	

tered edges instead of rabbeted edges. Cut a 45° miter along the 12" side of each side piece, making sure not to reduce the width of the pieces. Once all the miters are cut, proceed with the rest of the assembly.

9. Glue and nail all edges and assemble the four sides. Clamp tightly while the glue sets. Set all nails and fill the holes with wood putty before finishing.

10. Mount any light sockets and hangers on the top, then glue or nail in place.

11. Mount the bottom piece with screws; do not use nails, because you will have to have access to the inside to change the light bulb.

12. Finish as desired. If you like, colored plastic can be mounted inside the lantern with screws or glue to soften the lighting effect.

NOTE: Do *not* use plastic on top and bottom. (This would trap heat and cause a fire hazard.)

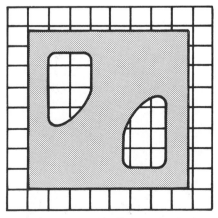

TOP AND BOTTOM TEMPLATE

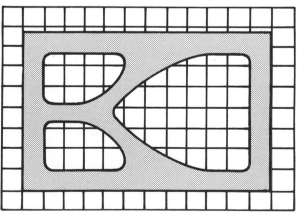

SIDE TEMPLATE

ONE SQUARE = 1"

GARDEN OR ENTRYWAY LAMP

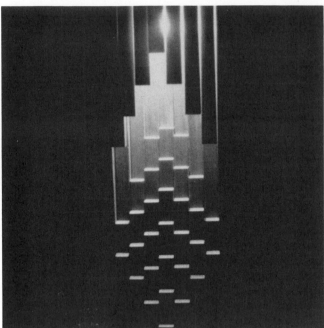

LIST OF MATERIALS

(finished dimensions in inches)

A	(25)	1-1/2 × 1-1/2 × 6
B	(1)	1-1/2 × 1-1/2 × 8
C	(2)	1-1/2 × 1-1/2 × 10
D	(1)	1-1/2 × 1-1/2 × 11
E	(2)	1-1/2 × 1-1/2 × 12
F	(2)	1-1/2 × 1-1/2 × 13
G	(4)	1-1/2 × 1-1/2 × 14
H	(2)	1-1/2 × 1-1/2 × 15
J	(2)	1-1/2 × 1-1/2 × 16
K	(5)	1-1/2 × 1-1/2 × 17
L	(2)	1-1/2 × 1-1/2 × 18
M	(2)	1-1/2 × 1-1/2 × 19
N	(3)	1-1/2 × 1-1/2 × 20
O	(2)	1-1/2 × 1-1/2 × 21
P	(2)	1-1/2 × 1-1/2 × 22
Q	(3)	1-1/2 × 1-1/2 × 23
R	(2)	1-1/2 × 1-1/2 × 25
S	(1)	1-1/2 × 1-1/2 × 26
T	(1)	1-1/2 × 1-1/2 × 38
U	(9)	1-1/2 × 1-1/2 × 48

Waterproof outlet box
Waterproof coupling
Light socket
UG wire
8d galvanized nails
#3 rebar
Waterproof glue

The design of this lamp is truly unique, and it is a deceptively easy project to build. The lamp is ideal for use in an entryway or garden. Keep in mind that any parts that come in contact with the ground should be made of redwood or pressure-treated lumber to provide resistance to decay.

1. Cut all pieces to length from 2 × 2 stock, following the dimensions given.

2. Cut a channel wide and deep enough to accommodate wiring down one side of the 38"-long piece (T).

3. Construct the individual rows using 8d galvanized nails and waterproof glue. Note that rows 1 through 4 are built in two sections.

4. Begin assembly by attaching row 6 to row 5, then add row 7 and row 8. Turn the assembly over and attach row 4, then row 3.

5. Install all electrical work at this point, being sure to follow all local electrical codes.

6. Attach rows, 9, 2, and 1.

7. Two 24"-long pieces of rebar can be used to hold the lamp in the ground. Drill holes in the bottom to accommodate the rebar, and hammer them into place.

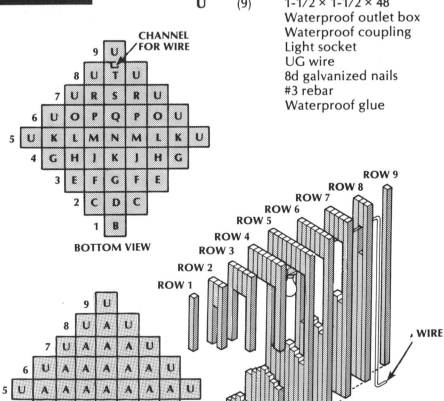

22

Molding and dowels are the main ingredients of these melodious wind chimes. The tones will vary according to the weight, length, and type of molding used, and dense hardwoods work best.

1. Cut the parts to size using the dimensions provided. The frame pieces (A, B) are made from shingle molding, while the chimes (D) in this example are different lengths of lattice molding.

2. Drill 1/4"-diameter holes 3/8" deep in the frame sides to accommodate the spindles (C). Drill five holes in each side, spacing them evenly.

3. Glue the spindles in place, then assemble the frame with brads and waterproof glue.

4. Attach small eye hooks at one end of each chime, and suspend the chimes from the frame with string. The distance between chimes should be far enough apart to allow them to swing freely, but close enough that they touch in a gentle breeze.

5. Finish as desired, then hang from your porch or a nearby tree.

LIST OF MATERIALS

(finished dimensions in inches)

A	Frame ends (2)	3/4 × 3/4 × 4 molding
B	Frame sides (2)	3/4 × 3/4 × 6 molding
C	Spindles (5)	1/4 dia. × 4 dowels
D	Chimes (12)	1/2 × 1/2 × varied lengths of lattice molding
	Eye hooks (12)	
	String	
	Brads	
	Waterproof glue	

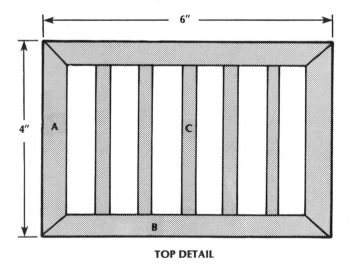

TOP DETAIL

NAPKIN HOLDER

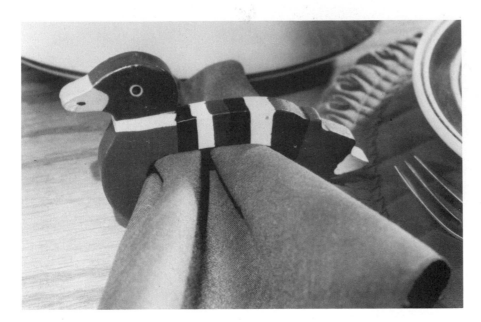

We used poplar to make this unique-looking napkin holder because it cuts easily, sands and finishes well, and is durable. If you plan to use a natural finish, you might want to use a different wood.

1. Transfer the pattern provided onto a 1/2″ × 5″ × 3″ piece of stock.

2. Use a scroll saw or jigsaw to cut out the duck shape.

3. Drill a starting hole at least 1/2″ in diameter through the body.

4. Feed the saw blade through the hole, mount and tension, and cut out the napkin hole.

5. Smooth the edges of the napkin hole with a small drum sander or a file.

6. Prime the holder with a good quality sealer, such as oil-based primer.

7. With a pencil, lightly draw the duck's features on the holder.

8. Hand paint, then spray with a clear, nontoxic finish to complete the project.

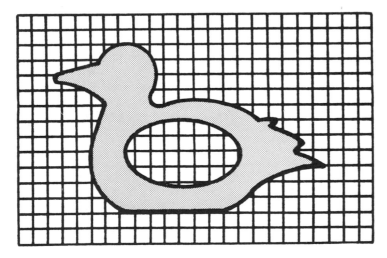

ONE SQUARE = 1/4″ **NAPKIN HOLDER TEMPLATE**

These shelf brackets are made with a scroll saw; use the pattern provided or design your own.

1. Cut the stock to 1-1/2″ × 6″ × 6-1/2″. This will be enough for two brackets.

2. Lay out the pattern on a piece of paper, then transfer it to the wood twice.

3. Drill a 1/2″-diameter hole in the center of each pattern.

4. Place the scroll saw blade through one of the holes and re-connect the blade. Tension the blade, lower the hold-down foot, and cut out the design.

5. Repeat steps 3 and 4 until the entire pattern is cut out. Do the same for the other pattern.

6. Cut the outside shape of each bracket.

7. If necessary, drum sand the edges of the brackets and finish as desired.

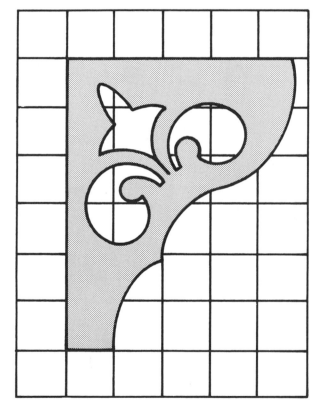

ONE SQUARE = 1″   **BRACKET PATTERN**

CANDLESTICKS

Use a round nose chisel to scrape the base to its final 4" diameter.

2. Using a 1/2" parting tool, cut the 3"-diameter "step" 7/16" from the faceplate. Use a skew chisel to scrape the bottom radius and a round nose chisel to scrape the curve and radius.

3. Sand the finished base on the lathe.

4. Mount the stock for the candlestick (B) between centers on the lathe. Use a gouge chisel to cut it round, and mark all length measurements on the cylinder.

5. Using a 1/2" part tool, mark the 3/4"-diameter × 3/4" section on the end of the candlestick that fits into the base. Use the skew chisel to turn the 3/4" diameter.

6. Cut the proper diameter measurements plus 1/16" at all pencil lines, then use skew and gouge chisels to cut the proper diameters.

7. Finish sand the candlestick. This can be used as the master for turning the second candlestick, as well as for future turnings.

8. Drill a 3/4"-diameter hole through the center of the base, then glue the candlestick to the base.

9. Drill the appropriate size hole for the candle. Finish as desired.

Candlesticks have always been a traditional American favorite, especially when they are made of cherry.

1. Use a bandsaw to cut a 4-1/4"-diameter circle from 3/4"-thick stock for the base (A). Mark the center for alignment on a lathe.

LIST OF MATERIALS

(finished dimensions in inches)

A	Bases (2)	4 dia. × 3/4
B	Candlesticks (2)	1-3/4 dia. × 5
	Wood glue	

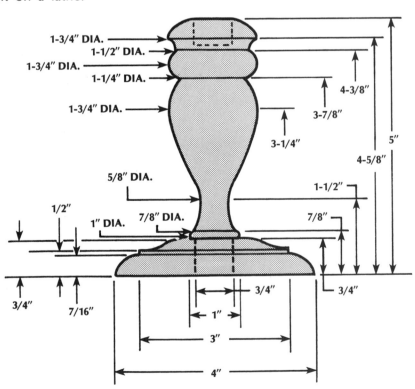

Although this octagonal hurricane lamp features a Christmas design and a 9-1/2" glass chimney, you aren't limited to these measurements or patterns. You can still follow the basic procedure and come up with your own design.

1. Cut all stock to size according to the dimensions given and bevel the sides to 22-1/2°.

2. Lay out the full size pattern, or design your own. Transfer the pattern to the outside of the sides (A).

3. Stack the sides together and secure with masking tape.

4. Drill a 3/8"-diameter hole in the center of each of the cutout designs. Place two sides at a time on a scroll saw and cut out the designs.

5. Remove the masking tape and sand the individual sides, if necessary.

6. Lay the sides flat and side-by-side, with the bevel sides down. Place two pieces of masking tape at each joint.

7. Carefully turn the taped assembly over so the bevel sides are facing up. Run a small bead of glue in each joint and on each end piece.

8. You can now roll up the assembly to form the octagonal lamp shape. Use a strap clamp or strong rubber bands around the top and bottom until the glue dries. Check for squareness.

9. Gently push the bottom (B) into the lamp until a depth of 1/4" has been reached on all sides.

10. Install the glue blocks (C) on alternating sides to hold the bottom in place. When the glue dries, do any necessary finish sanding.

11. Finish the outside of the lamp as desired. Paint the inside with a high-gloss white paint, or cover the cutouts with different colored pieces of cellophane.

12. Cut a wood circle (D) to fit loosely inside the bottom of the chimney. Drill a hole in it to accept the candle. Fasten into the bottom of the lamp.

13. Install the glass chimney and candle.

LIST OF MATERIALS

(finished dimensions in inches)

A	Sides (8)	1/4 × 4 × 11-1/2
B	Bottom	1/4 × 9 × 9
C	Glue blocks (4)	1/4 × 1/4 × 4
D	Candle holder	1-3/4 dia. × 7/8
	Glass chimney	
	Wood glue	

HOLE DRILLED TO FIT CANDLE

1-3/4"

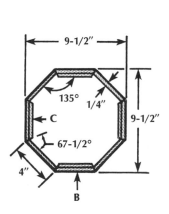

9-1/2"

135°

1/4"

C

67-1/2°

9-1/2"

4"

B

ONE SQUARE = 1"

SIDE PATTERN

These puzzles are great fun for little hands. And if our dog, cat, and dinosaur designs don't suit your fancy, just use your imagination and come up with your own.

1. Transfer the patterns to the proper size stock.

2. Using a scroll saw, bandsaw, or jigsaw, cut the outside shape of the puzzles, then the inside lines.

3. Lay out the legs on the scrap pieces left over from the previous cuts. Cut out these pieces.

4. Hand file and sand the puzzles. Color with food coloring, then surface coat with a nontoxic finish.

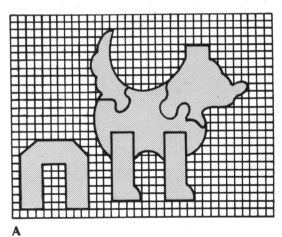

A

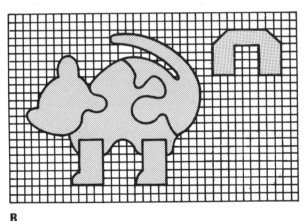

B

ONE SQUARE = 1/4"

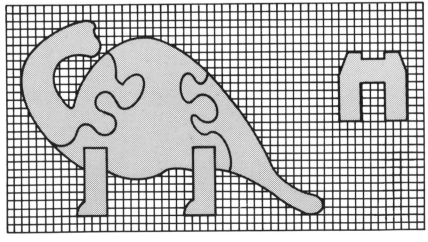

C

LIST OF MATERIALS

(finished dimensions in inches)

A	Dog	3/4 × 5-1/2 × 5-1/4
B	Cat	3/4 × 5 × 7-3/4
C	Dinosaur	3/4 × 8-1/4 × 9-3/4

Aromatic red cedar ornaments serve two purposes. First, they provide one of nature's finest aromas for your Christmas tree, be it real or artificial. Second, they add a clean, woodsy fragrance to closets and drawers. Best of all, red cedar lasts forever—light sanding renews its natural oils and fragrance.

BUTTERFLY AND BEAR

1. Lay out the full size patterns on a piece of paper, then transfer them to a 1/4" or 1/2"-thick piece of red cedar.
2. Cut out the patterns using a scroll saw or jigsaw.
3. Sand all edges and surfaces as needed.

BELL

1. Lay out the full size pattern on a piece of paper, then transfer it to a 1/4" × 5" × 5" piece of red cedar.
2. Drill a 3/16"-diameter hole in the center of the area to be cut out.
3. Place the scroll saw or jigsaw blade through the hole, lower the hold-down foot, and cut out the design.
4. Using a 1/16" bit, drill a hole through the top of the outer circle and in the top of the bell.
5. Attach the bell to the outer circle with a 4" length of black upholstery thread; a small amount of glue can be used to secure the thread to the bell and circle.
6. Attach the thread to an ornament hook.

LIST OF MATERIALS

(finished dimensions in inches)

A	Butterfly	1/4 or 1/2 × 3 × 2-1/8
B	Bear	1/4 or 1/2 × 2-5/8 × 3-1/4
C	Bell	1/4 × 4 × 4
	Black upholstery thread	
	Ornament hooks	
	Wood glue	

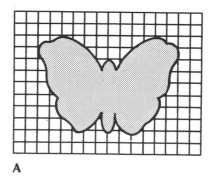

A

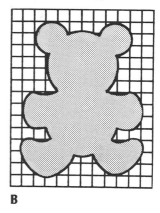

B

ONE SQUARE = 1/4"

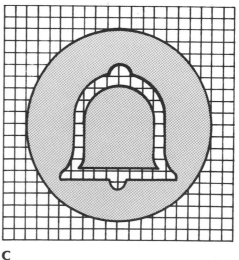

C

This combination of mirror and planter is a unique addition to any room in your home. Use the specially made fixture and the pin routing technique if you plan to build several; for only one or two, use a jigsaw. Clear pine was used in this example.

MAKING THE FIXTURE

1. Trace the pattern provided on a piece of 1/2" plywood.
2. Use a saber saw or jigsaw to cut out the design.
3. Tack or screw the plywood pattern to the particleboard side of a 12" × 28" piece of plastic-laminated particleboard. The straight, bottom edge of the pattern must be aligned perfectly with the bottom edge of the cutout.
4. Insert a 3/8"-diameter pin in the router arm table, aligning it with a 3/8"-diameter straight flute, carbide tip router bit. Set the depth-stop rod to rout a 3/8"-deep groove.
5. Flip the fixture over and trace around all the routed-out areas on the pattern, cutting a 3/8"-deep groove in the laminate side of the fixture. Make a groove at the top of the fixture for the top edge of the planter.
6. When all the grooves have been cut, flip the fixture over and remove the plywood pattern.
7. Drill four 11/64"-diameter screw holes through the fixture at the points indicated. Countersink the laminate side of the holes so the heads of #8 screws will be completely recessed when inserted. This completes the fixture.

MAKING THE MIRROR WITH PLANTER

1. Attach the 3/4" × 11-1/8" × 28" workpiece to the particleboard side of the fixture with #8 × 1" wood screws.
2. Again using the 3/8"-diameter pin and 3/8"-diameter bit, align the pin and bit perfectly. Set the depth-stop rod so the bit barely cuts through the workpiece.
3. Turn the fixture over and guide the pin through all the grooves, transferring the design to the attached workpiece. To avoid forcing the bit through the workpiece too rapidly, make at least three cuts in each area.
4. Change to a chamfering rounding-over bit and "dress" the edges of each cutout area.
5. Cut out the pieces for the planter according to the dimensions given. Cut the 15° angles on the sides (C) as shown, and bevel the front (A) to match the dimensions.
6. Nail the two sides to the back (D) with the 15° beveled edges away from the piece and the widest part of the bevel at the top.
7. Nail the front to the sides, then nail the bottom (B) in place. Recess

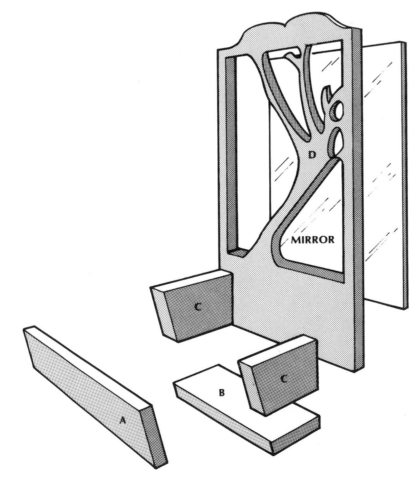

LIST OF MATERIALS (Planter)

(finished dimensions in inches)

A	Front	3/4 × 4-11/16 × 11-1/8
B	Bottom	3/4 × 5 × 11-1/8
C	Sides (2)	3/4 × 4-5/16 × 5-3/8
D	Back	3/4 × 11-1/8 × 26-5/8
	Mirror	10 × 19-1/4
	Flathead wood screws	#8 × 1
	3d finishing nails	
	Glazier's points	
	Wood putty	
	Waterproof wood glue	

all nail heads as you go; they can be filled with wood putty after the assembly is complete.

8. The best method of securing the mirror is to recess the entire mirror (1/4" deep) area in the back using a 3/4" router bit. Square the corners with a chisel. Lay the mirror in the recess and secure with glazier's points.

9. To hang the mirror/planter, use two wood screws and ordinary picture hanging wire.

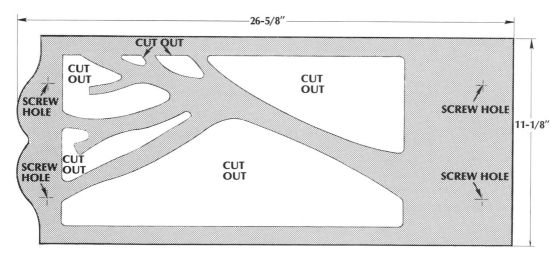

SIDE DETAIL

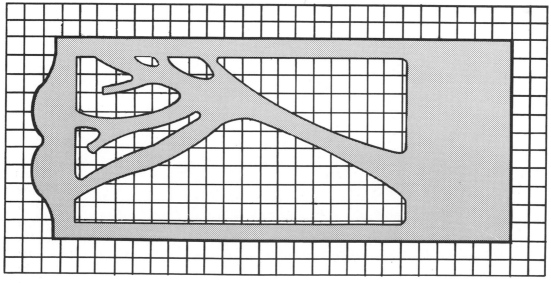

SIDE PATTERN

ONE SQUARE = 1"

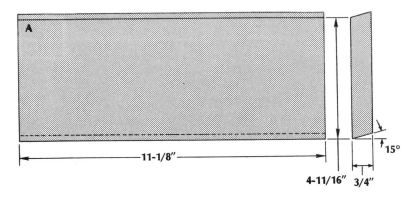

11-1/8″

15°

4-11/16″ 3/4″

FRONT DETAIL

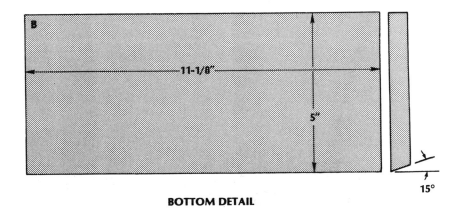

11-1/8″

5″

15°

BOTTOM DETAIL

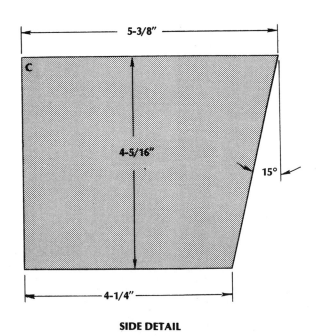

5-3/8″

4-5/16″

15°

4-1/4″

SIDE DETAIL

Elegant and simple, with a touch of Oriental serenity, this divider screen creates privacy in the house or garden. Although the screen in this example has three panels, you can make it any size you choose.
1. Cut all the pieces to size according to the dimensions provided.

LIST OF MATERIALS

(finished dimensions in inches)
A Inside stiles (4)   3/4 × 1-3/4 × 72
B Outside stiles (2)   3/4 × 3-1/2 × 72
C Rails (12)   3/4 × 3-1/2 × 15-1/4
D Panels (12)   1/8 × 16 × 16 fiberglass
      Molding (36)   1/4 × 3/8 × 16
      Double action hinges
      Dowels
      Fine brass nails
      Wood glue

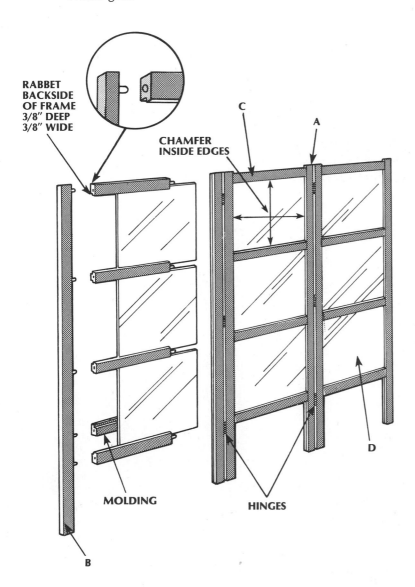

RABBET BACKSIDE OF FRAME 3/8" DEEP 3/8" WIDE

CHAMFER INSIDE EDGES

C   A

MOLDING

HINGES

B

D

2. On the backside of each rail (C), cut a 3/8" × 3/8" rabbet along the top and bottom edge. (Note that the three top rails require rabbets only along the bottom edge, while the three bottom rails require rabbets only along the top edge.)
3. Assemble the frames by connecting the stiles (A, B) and rails with dowels and glue as shown, leaving 15-1/4" between rails.
4. Round over or chamfer the vertical edges of the openings on the front side of the rails. Round over the other edges of the frame as desired.
5. Sand and finish at this time; it will be much more difficult to do after the panels (D) have been inserted.
6. Insert the panels in the rabbets. Miter the molding pieces to fit inside the rabbets and hold the panels in place. Attach the molding with fine brass nails, being careful not to split the molding or panel.
7. Attach double action hinges and connect the frames to complete the screen.

STACKING BOXES

If you've ever had trouble getting the kids to keep their rooms straightened up, you'll love this project. These simple, stackable plywood boxes can be formed into endless combinations, including open-ended, two-tiered, and divided into drawers. The instructions and dimensions that follow are for one open-ended box; build as many as you want, and change the dimensions where it will better suit your needs.

1. Cut the parts to size according to the dimensions provided. Use notches as shown for ease of assembly.

2. Cut a 1" × 4" handle in each door.

3. Sand the parts thoroughly, using wood filler where necessary to cover imperfections.

4. Assemble with 2d finishing nails, glue, and wrap-around hinges. Either mortise the hinges into the plywood or trim the width of the door as needed to allow for the hinge thickness.

5. Attach the doorstop (E) to the inside of panel B.

6. Install magnetic catches.

LIST OF MATERIALS

(finished dimensions in inches)

A	Top and bottom (2)	1/2 × 17-3/4 × 17-3/4 plywood
B	Sides (2)	1/2 × 17-3/4 × 17-3/4 plywood
C	Back	1/2 × 17 × 17 plywood
D	Door	1/2 × 16-5/8 × 16-5/8 plywood
E	Doorstop	1/2 × 1/2 × 16-3/4 pine
	2d finishing nails	
	Wrap-around hinges (2)	
	Magnetic catches	
	Wood glue	

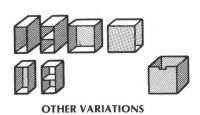

OTHER VARIATIONS

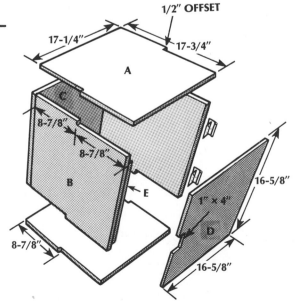

1/2" OFFSET

17-1/4" 17-3/4"

8-7/8"

8-7/8"

8-7/8"

16-5/8"

16-5/8"

1" × 4"

Accents and Accessories

From a rustic log cradle to an elegant coffee table with mirrored top, the projects in this section will enhance your entire home. They are designed to be as practical as they are attractive, and you're sure to enjoy building them as much as your family will enjoy using them.

LOG CRADLE

Carrying and storing firewood can be messy and cumbersome, but here's something to make the chore a lot easier: a log cradle. It takes up less than three square feet of floor space, despite all the firewood it holds. Build it from rough-cut lumber for a rustic touch, or use smooth stock for a more modern look.

1. Cut the pieces to size according to the dimensions given.

2. Drill two 3/8"-diameter holes in each spreader (D) as shown.

3. Attach two legs (A) to each rail (B) using 6d finishing nails and glue. Mark an 8-3/4" radius on the inside of the leg-and-rail assemblies, then cut the contours on a bandsaw or jigsaw. After cutting, sand the machined edges smooth.

4. Starting in the center, nail the slats (C) in place as shown. Use a 3/4" piece of scrap as a spacer.

5. Thread one end of a rope through each spreader. Leave a slight loop behind each spreader for a handle, then nail the rope in place with 6d finishing nails.

6. Set all nails below the surface and fill the holes with filler. Finish with spar varnish or another good outdoor finish.

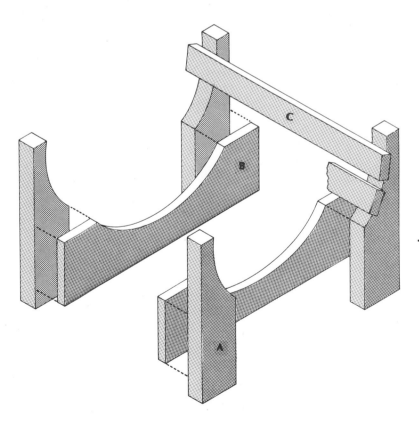

LIST OF MATERIALS

(finished dimensions in inches)

A	Legs (4)	1-1/2 × 3-1/2 × 15
B	Rails (2)	3/4 × 5-1/4 × 20
C	Slats (9)	3/4 × 2-1/4 × 20
D	Spreaders (2)	3/4 × 1-1/2 × 14
	Rope	3/8 dia. × 80
	6d finishing nails	
	Filler	
	Wood glue	

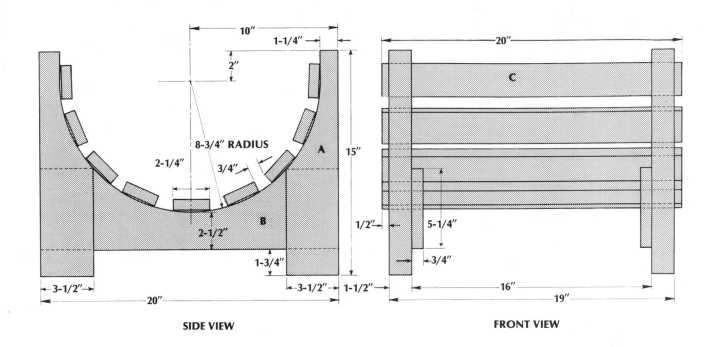

SIDE VIEW

FRONT VIEW

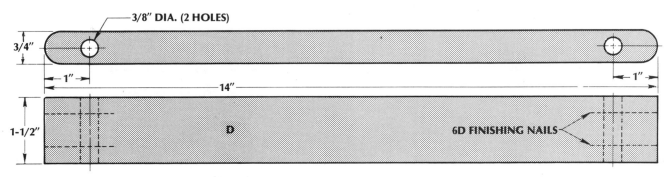

SPREADER DETAIL

HANGING DOUBLE PLANTER

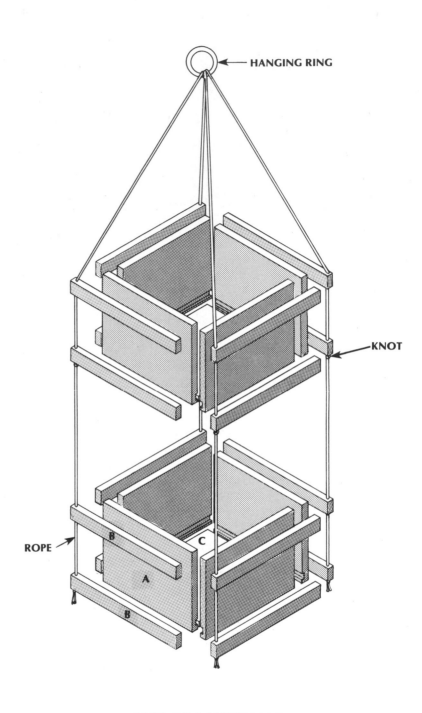

HANGING RING

KNOT

ROPE

Filled with garden greenery, this double planter can be used indoors or out. It's an attractive hanging showcase for your plants, and it can be easily constructed with redwood. If you have a knack with macramé hangers, you might want to design your own cord work around the two boxes.

1. The entire planter can be made from a single 12' length of 1 × 12. Begin by cutting the bottoms (C) to length.

2. Rip the remaining lumber to a width of 9-1/4" to provide stock for the sides (A). Cut each of the sides to length; there should be sufficient scrap left for the frame (B).

3. Rip the frame stock to 1-1/2" wide, then cut all 16 pieces to length.

4. Cut a 3/4"-wide × 3/8"-deep groove 1/4" above the bottom edge of each of the sides.

5. Drill one hole in each frame piece to accommodate the rope being used. Drill two 1/2"-diameter drainage holes in the bottom as shown.

6. To assemble, attach three of the sides with glue and finishing nails. Then slide the bottom in place, but do not glue it. Attach the fourth

LIST OF MATERIALS

(finished dimensions in inches)

A	Sides (8)	3/4 × 9-1/4 × 11-1/4
B	Frame pieces (16)	3/4 × 1-1/2 × 13-1/2
C	Bottoms (2)	3/4 × 11-1/4 × 11-1/4
	Rope	3/16 or 1/4 dia.
	Hanging ring	
	4d finishing nails	
	Water-resistant wood glue	

side to hold the bottom. Repeat for the second box.

7. When the glue has dried, sand all corner joints smooth. Attach the frame pieces around the boxes, one side at a time.

8. Countersink all nails and fill the holes with filler.

9. Finish with a good outdoor finish, then string on a rope and hanging ring to complete the planter.

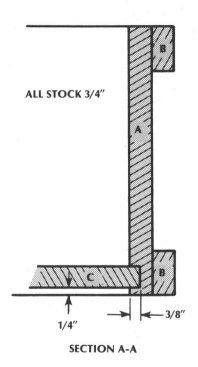

ALL STOCK 3/4"

1/4" — 3/8"

SECTION A-A

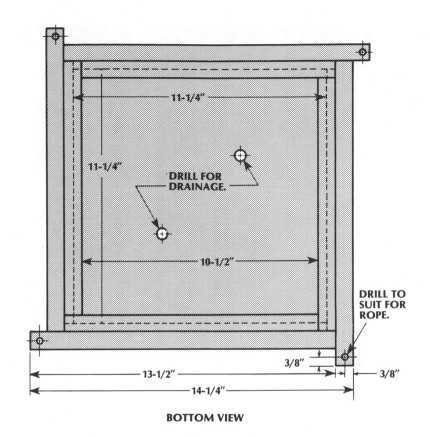

11-1/4"

11-1/4"

DRILL FOR DRAINAGE.

10-1/2"

DRILL TO SUIT FOR ROPE.

3/8"

13-1/2"

14-1/4"

3/8"

BOTTOM VIEW

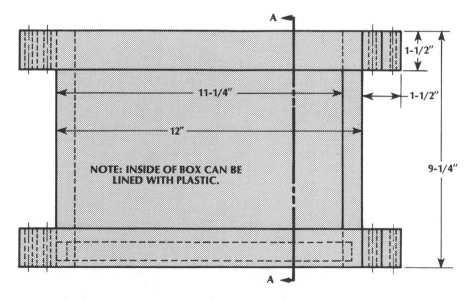

1-1/2"

11-1/4"

1-1/2"

12"

NOTE: INSIDE OF BOX CAN BE LINED WITH PLASTIC.

9-1/4"

A

A

FRONT VIEW

This cathedral-style wine rack holds five bottles of wine horizontally, and it can also be carried for convenience. It's a snap to make several at a time by pin routing; a saber saw or jigsaw can be used if you are making only one or two.

MAKING THE FIXTURE

1. Transfer the pattern to a piece of 1/2" plywood.

2. Use a bandsaw, saber saw, or jigsaw to cut out the shape.

3. Nail the template to the particleboard side of a piece of laminated countertop material.

4. Working with a 1/4" to 1/2" straight bit and a matching pin, pin rout a groove in the laminate. Make the first pass cutting only 1/8" into the laminate, drop the router 1/8" lower on the second pass, and continue until the groove is 3/8" to 1/2" deep.

5. Drill and countersink the template for nails to attach the workpiece. Locate the nails so the holes will not detract from the appearance of the finished wine rack; a good spot is where you will later drill for dowels.

6. Attach a 3/4" × 10" × 18" workpiece to the template with nails. Pin rout the workpiece, letting the pin follow the groove in the template. Do not try to cut all the way through on the first pass; do it 1/4" or less at a time.

7. When the pin routing has been completed, drill three 1"-diameter holes in each of the rack ends as shown.

8. Cut three 1"-diameter × 8-1/2"-long dowels. Sand all the pieces.

9. Assemble the wine rack with wood glue, then stain and/or finish to suit.

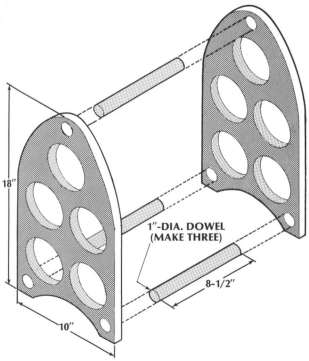

1"-DIA. DOWEL
(MAKE THREE)

18"

10"

8-1/2"

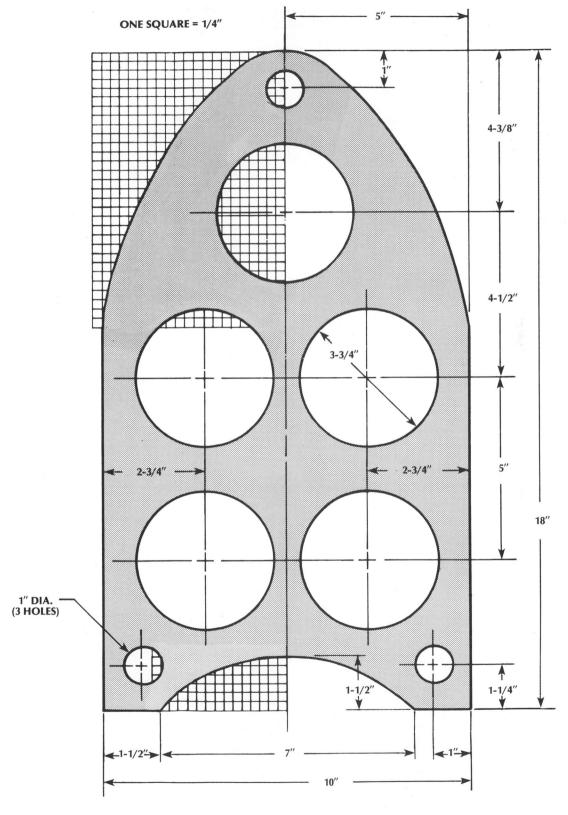

ONE SQUARE = 1/4"

1" DIA.
(3 HOLES)

TEMPLATE LAYOUT

MIRRORED COFFEE TABLE

LIST OF MATERIALS

(finished dimensions in inches)

A	Frame sides (2)	1-1/2 × 2-1/2 × 30-3/4
B	Frame ends (2)	1-1/2 × 2-1/2 × 18-3/4
C	Legs (4)	1-1/2 × 2-1/2 × 18
D	Apron sides (2)	1-1/2 × 2-1/2 × 25
E	Apron ends (2)	1-1/2 × 2-1/2 × 15
	Flathead wood screws	#8 × 1-1/4
	Bronzed mirror	1/4 × 13-5/8 × 25-5/8
	Dowels	1/2 dia. × 2
	Wood putty	
	3d finishing nails	
	Wood glue	

This handsome table features a bronzed mirror set in the top. You may want to put glides on the bottom of the legs to protect your floor or carpet.

1. After cutting all of the pieces to size, cut a 1/4" × 3/8" rabbet in the frame sides (A) and ends (B) to accommodate the mirror.

2. Cut 45° miters on the frame sides and ends, and assemble by gluing and nailing. Set the nails slightly below the surface and fill with putty.

3. Cut curves on the legs (C). A one-pound coffee can was used in this example, but you can use any small round object that gives you a curve you like.

4. Attach the legs to the apron pieces (D, E) with glue and dowels, making sure the assembly is square.

5. Center the frame on the leg/apron assembly, rabbeted side up, and attach it with counterbored screws inserted from underneath into the frame.

6. Sand and finish the entire table.

7. Set the mirror into the rabbet. Be sure to protect the edge of the mirror from water because the silver in the mirror can tarnish.

NOTE: When ordering the glass, make sure that it is tempered and specify that the edges be ground.

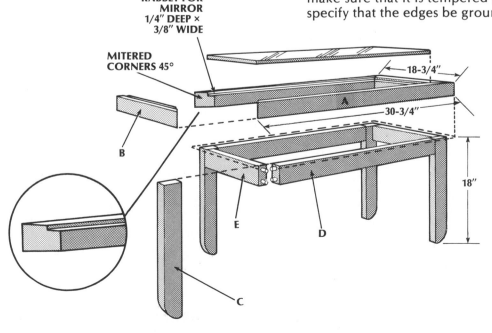

RABBET FOR MIRROR 1/4" DEEP × 3/8" WIDE

MITERED CORNERS 45°

18-3/4"

30-3/4"

18"

This impressive table and matching bench are perfect for family dining, arts and crafts, and other group projects. The originals were made of 5/4 redwood, but you can use any good quality wood.

1. Glue up 5/4 × 8 stock for cutting the tabletop (A) and bench top (F) pieces. After the glue has dried, sand the panels flat and cut them to the listed dimensions.

2. Construct the leg assemblies by gluing and doweling the legs (B, G) and side rails (C, H) together. Clamp tightly, making sure each leg assembly is square.

3. Drill holes in the back and front rails (D, J) for attaching the leg assemblies. Rout all exposed edges with a 3/8"-radius quarter rounding bit before assembling.

4. Attach the leg assemblies to the back and front rails with dowels and glue. Check for squareness.

5. Install the corner braces (E, K) with flathead wood screws.

6. Attach the tops to the bases with roundhead wood screws and washers. Note the 5/8" setback for the side rails on both the bench and table.

7. To complete the project, sand the table and bench and finish as desired.

LIST OF MATERIALS

(finished dimensions in inches)

A	Tabletop	1-1/8 × 36-1/2 × 70
B	Table legs (4)	1-1/8 × 3-1/2 × 28-1/2
C	Table side rails (2)	1-1/8 × 3-1/2 × 29
D	Table back and front rails (2)	1-1/8 × 3-1/2 × 66-1/2
E	Table corner braces (4)	1-1/8 × 3-1/2 × 11
F	Bench top	1-1/8 × 14-1/2 × 66
G	Bench legs (4)	1-1/8 × 3-1/2 × 15-1/2
H	Bench side rails (2)	1-1/8 × 3-1/2 × 7
J	Bench back and front rails (2)	1-1/8 × 3-1/2 × 62-1/2
K	Bench corner braces (2)	1-1/8 × 3-1/2 × 10-1/2
	Dowels	
	Flathead wood screws	
	Roundhead wood screws and washers	
	Wood glue	

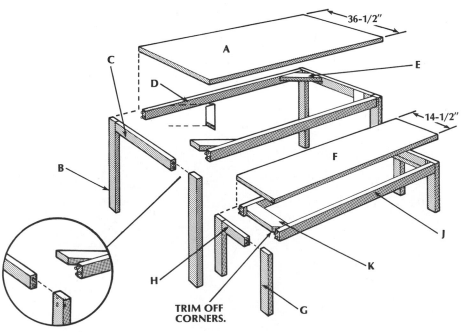

TRIM OFF CORNERS.

DESK/WORKBENCH

Good quality plywood is all that's needed to build this sturdy desk/workbench. No nails, screws, or glue are required; the secret of the assembly is the interlocking slots.

1. Mark off all measurements on the plywood as indicated in the diagram. If cutting with a handsaw, lay out the dimensions with the good side up; if using a circular or saber saw, lay out the dimensions on the back of the plywood to prevent chipping.

2. Begin by cutting off the 33" section; then divide it into the legs (A).

3. Rip the remaining sheet for the leg brace (B), back brace (C), and top (D). Round all the corners to a 2-1/2" radius using a coping or saber saw.

4. Cut the 3/4" slots as indicated in the diagram, sawing to the inside line of the slots for a snug fit. Use a piece of scrap plywood to check the width of each slot as you go. Use a wood rasp or sandpaper to enlarge slightly undersized slots.

5. Assemble by dropping the legs onto the leg brace slots, installing the back brace, and finally setting the top in place.

6. For a natural finish, band the edges of the plywood with matching 3/4" wood tape. For a painted desk/workbench, use either wood tape or fill the edges with putty. Sand smooth, prime with oil-based primer, then paint.

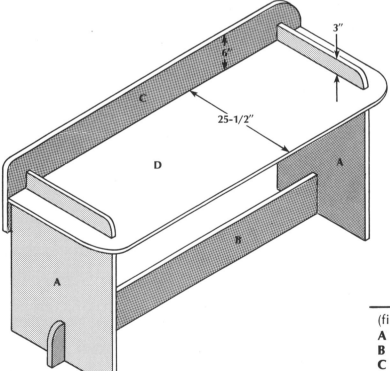

LIST OF MATERIALS

(finished dimensions in inches)

A	Legs (2)	3/4 × 24 × 33 plywood
B	Leg brace	3/4 × 7 × 63 plywood
C	Back brace	3/4 × 14 × 63 plywood
D	Top	3/4 × 27 × 63 plywood

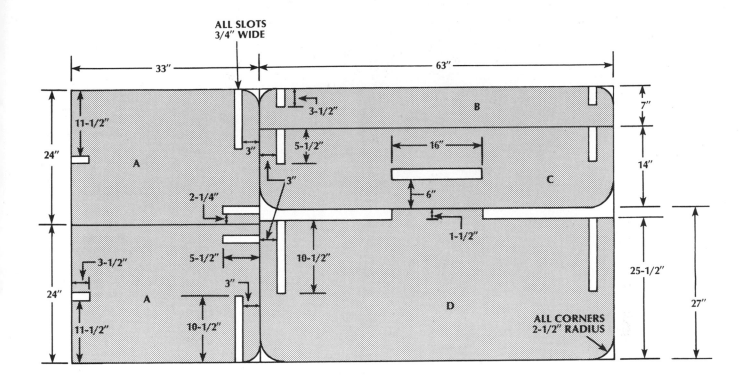

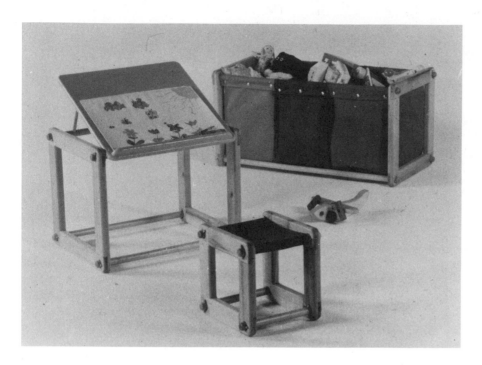

Everyone needs a place to work and to store their own "tools of the trade," and children are no exception. These three pieces, constructed of 5/4 material, have been designed especially for children ages 3 to 7; they each utilize the same basic end frame construction. The desk features supports that allow for a dual-position top: either flat or propped up to form a mini drawing board. The stool is sturdy enough to withstand playtime abuse, but still light enough so that a child can pick it up and move it. Finally, the top chest offers space to store a room full of toys and games. And all three pieces can be disassembled quickly and redesigned to suit your child's particular needs.

DESK

1. Begin by cutting all parts to size according to the dimensions given.
2. Cut half laps on both ends of all end frame pieces (A). Alternate the half laps by cutting one on the top of each piece and the other on the bottom as shown.
3. Glue and clamp the end frames together. Cut a 1" radius at the corners and a 1/4" radius on all edges. Sand and drill 1"-diameter holes as shown.
4. Draw two lines lengthwise and 90° apart on each of the cross members (B). Along one of the lines on each cross member measure in 1/2" from each end and mark. Along the other line measure in 1-7/8" from each end and mark.
5. Drill a 1/4"-diameter hole all the way through the cross members at each of the marks. These holes are needed to accommodate the end frame pins (E).
6. On one of the cross members, measure in 4-1/4" from both ends of one line and mark. At these

marks drill 1/2"-diameter × 3/4"-deep holes to accommodate the top supports (F).
7. Chamfer both ends of the cross members and end frame pins, and one end of each top support. Sand all pieces.
8. On the back side of the top (C), drill two 9/16"-diameter × 1/4"-deep holes to accommodate the top supports and two 1/8"-diameter × 1/2"-deep holes to accommodate the conduit clamps.
9. Cut a 1" radius on the corners of the top, and a 1/4" radius around all edges. Sand the top.
10. Cut a 1" radius on both ends of the pencil holder (D), then glue it in place on the top.
11. Insert the cross members through the holes in the end frames and secure with the end frame pins.
12. Glue the top supports into the holes in the cross member.
13. Place the top over the frame and secure with conduit clamps and screws as shown.
14. Finish the desk as desired.

STOOL

1. Cut all of the parts to size according to the dimensions provided.
2. Cut half laps on both ends of all end frame pieces (A). Alternate the half laps by cutting one on the top of each piece and the other on the bottom as shown.
3. Glue and clamp the end frames together. Cut a 1" radius at the corners and a 1/4" radius on all
(continued on page 50)

LIST OF MATERIALS (Desk)

(finished dimensions in inches)

A	End frame pieces (8)	5/4 × 2-1/2 × 18
B	Cross members (4)	1-dia. × 24 dowels
C	Top	3/4 × 20 × 20-1/4 particleboard
D	Pencil holder	3/4 × 1 × 19 particleboard
E	End frame pins (16)	1/4-dia. × 1-3/4 dowels
F	Top supports (2)	1/2-dia. × 7-3/4 dowels
	Conduit clamps and screws (2)	
	Wood glue	

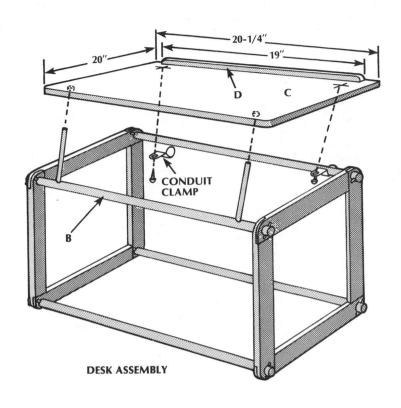

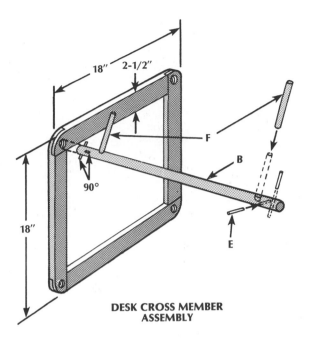

DESK ASSEMBLY

CONDUIT CLAMP

DESK CROSS MEMBER ASSEMBLY

90°

LIST OF MATERIALS (Stool)

(finished dimensions in inches)

A	End frame pieces (8)	5/4 × 2-1/2 × 12
B	Cross members (4)	1-dia. × 12 dowels
C	End frame pins (16)	1/4-dia. × 1-3/4 dowels
	Nonstretch seat fabric	10 × 24-1/2

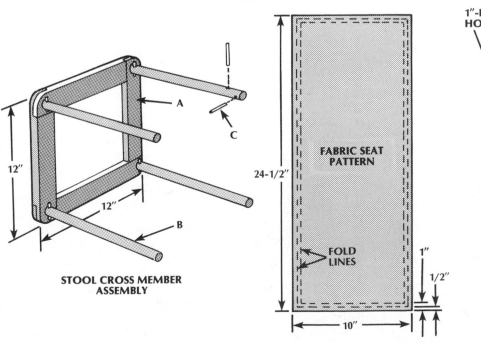

STOOL CROSS MEMBER ASSEMBLY

FABRIC SEAT PATTERN

24-1/2″

FOLD LINES

10″

1″

1/2″

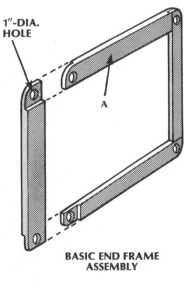

1″-DIA. HOLE

BASIC END FRAME ASSEMBLY

edges. Sand and drill 1"-diameter holes as shown.

4. Draw two lines lengthwise and 90° apart on each of the cross members (B). Along one of the lines on each cross member measure in 1/2" from each end and mark. Along the other line measure in 1-7/8" from each end and mark.

5. Drill a 1/4"-diameter hole all the way through the cross members at each of the marks. These holes are needed to accommodate the end frame pins (C).

6. Chamfer the ends of the cross members and end frame pins; then sand.

7. Do any finishing now; it can dry while the seat cover is being made.

8. After cutting the seat fabric to size, draw a fold line 1" from the edge of the fabric. Fold over all edges to the line, then fold again to form a 1/2" hem around the perimeter of the seat. Pin and sew.

9. Bring the two 8" sewn ends together, overlapping them 1/4", and again pin and sew.

10. Insert the cross members through the holes in one of the end frames and secure with end frame pins.

11. Slip the seat cover over the cross members, then insert the cross members through the holes in the other end frame. Secure with end frame pins.

TOY CHEST

1. Cut all of the parts to size using the dimensions given.

2. Cut half laps on both ends of all end frame pieces (A). Alternate the half laps by cutting one on the top of each piece and the other on the bottom as shown.

3. Glue and clamp the end frames together. Cut a 1" radius at the corners and a 1/4" radius on all edges. Sand and drill 1"-diameter holes as shown.

4. Draw two lines lengthwise and 90° apart on each of the cross members (B). Along one of the lines on each cross member, mea-

LIST OF MATERIALS (Toy Chest)

(finished dimensions in inches)

A	End frame pieces (8)	5/4 × 2-1/2 × 18
B	Cross members (4)	1-dia. × 36 dowels
C	End frame pins (16)	1/4-dia. × 1-3/4 dowels
D	Bottoms (3)	1/4 × 10-1/2 × 14-1/4 plywood
	Nonstretch fabric (3)	13 × 54
	Nonstretch fabric (6)	17 × 17
	#24 snaps (18)	

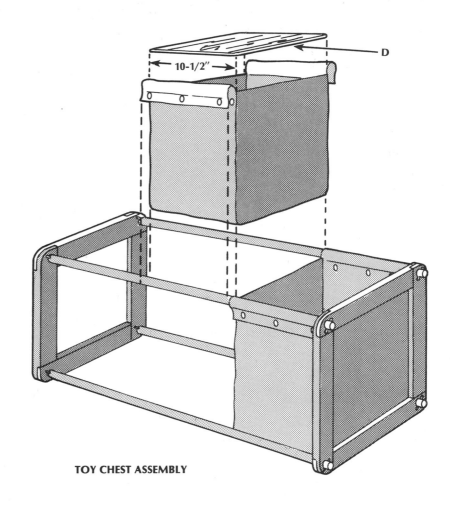

TOY CHEST ASSEMBLY

sure in 1/2" from each end and mark. Along the other line, measure in 1-7/8" from each end and mark.

5. Drill a 1/4"-diameter hole all the way through the cross members at each of the marks. These holes are needed to accommodate the end frame pins (C).

6. Chamfer the ends of the cross members and end frame pins; then sand.

7. Smooth the edges of the bottoms (D); then sand.

8. Cut the fabric for the bottom and side panels to size. Draw a fold line 1" in from the edges of each piece. Do the same with the fabric for the end panels.

9. Fold one edge of the end panels over to the 1" line, then fold it over again to create a 1/2" hem. Pin and sew; this will form the top edge of the end panels.

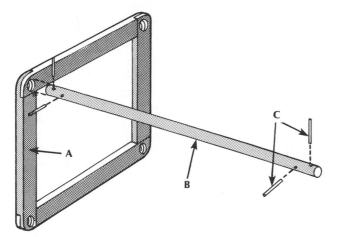

TOY CHEST DOWEL ASSEMBLY

10. Pin the end and side panels together for each pouch. Sew the pieces together, being sure to leave a 1/2" hem. The finished flaps should be 3-1/2" long.

11. Fold the pouches right side out to measure the locations for the snaps. Holding the snaps in position, use a nail to punch three holes through the flap and side. Fasten three snap sets in the holes, then repeat the procedure for all the flaps.

12. Insert the cross members through the holes in the end frames, and secure with end frame pins.

13. Attach the pouches by wrapping the flaps around the cross members and snapping them shut.

14. Finally, set the bottoms into the pouches.

15. Finish as desired.

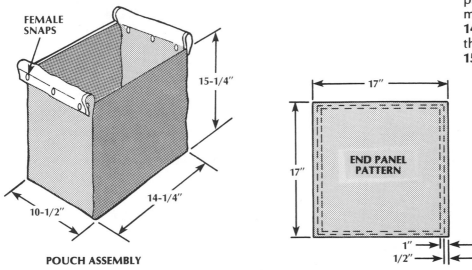

POUCH ASSEMBLY

FEMALE SNAPS

15-1/4"

14-1/4"

10-1/2"

17"

17"

END PANEL PATTERN

1"

1/2"

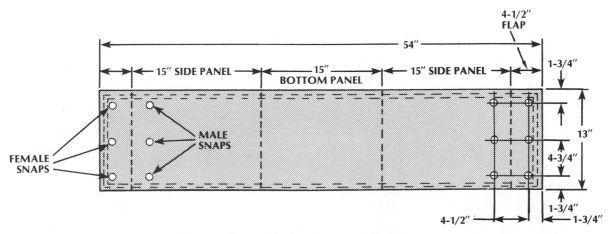

BOTTOM AND SIDE PANEL PATTERN

54"

15" SIDE PANEL

15" BOTTOM PANEL

15" SIDE PANEL

4-1/2" FLAP

1-3/4"

13"

4-3/4"

1-3/4"

4-1/2"

1-3/4"

MALE SNAPS

FEMALE SNAPS

Y ou can keep your cassette tapes safe and dry in this handsome walnut case. It's perfect for home or car and makes a great gift for music lovers.

1. Cut all of the parts to size following the dimensions provided.

2. Lay out a template for the curved track of the door as shown in the detail drawing. Cut out with a bandsaw and sand to size.

3. Using a 1/4"-diameter guide pin on the router arm and a 1/4"-diameter straight bit, set the depth of the cutter to 1/4". Use carpet tape to fasten the template (cut in the previous step) to the top (A), then rout the door groove. Repeat for the bottom (A).

4. Cut 1/2"-wide × 1/4"-deep rabbets in the top, bottom, right end (B), and left end (G).

5. Cut a 1/8"-deep groove as shown in the top and bottom to accommodate the Masonite reinforcement plate (E).

6. Pin three strips of tape 2" apart on a flat surface, making sure they are straight and parallel. Run a small bead of glue on each strip. Place the door pieces (F) perpendicular to the strips and parallel to each other on the strips. Allow 30 minutes to dry.

7. Unpin the tape strips and place them over a curved surface, making sure no two pieces of wood are stuck together. Remove any excess glue and trim the excess tape.

8. Rout a 3/8" ogee on the edge of the end cap (C) as shown.

9. Sand all parts, then apply one coat of finish to each. Be careful not to get any finish on the rabbets in the top and bottom pieces.

10. Using a disc sander, radius the end of the reinforcement plate.

11. Place a small amount of wax in the grooves in the top and bottom, then dry assemble all parts. The door should slide easily.

12. Using the glue sparingly, do the final assembly. Clamp and check for squareness and door operation.

13. Sand and finish the outside of the case, then attach the knob.

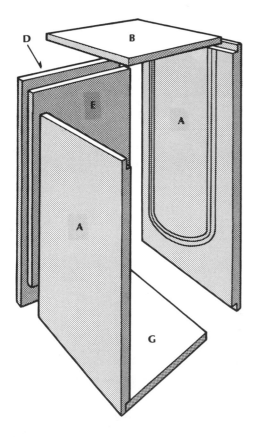

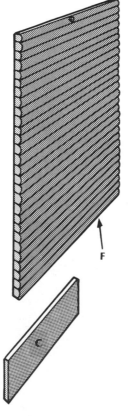

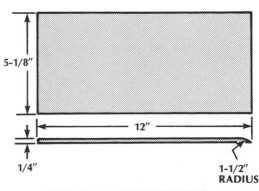

REINFORCEMENT PLATE DETAIL

5-1/8"

12"

1/4"

1-1/2" RADIUS

LIST OF MATERIALS

(finished dimensions in inches)

A	Top and bottom (2)	1/2 × 5 × 14
B	Right end	1/2 × 5 × 5-1/4
C	End cap	3/8 × 2-1/4 × 4-3/4
D	Back	1/2 × 5-1/4 × 13-1/2
E	Reinforcement plate	1/8 × 5-1/4 × 12 Masonite
F	Door pieces (30)	1/4 × 1/2 × 5-1/4
G	Left end	1/2 × 5 × 5-1/4
	Carpet tape	
	Knob	1/2 dia.
	Wood glue	

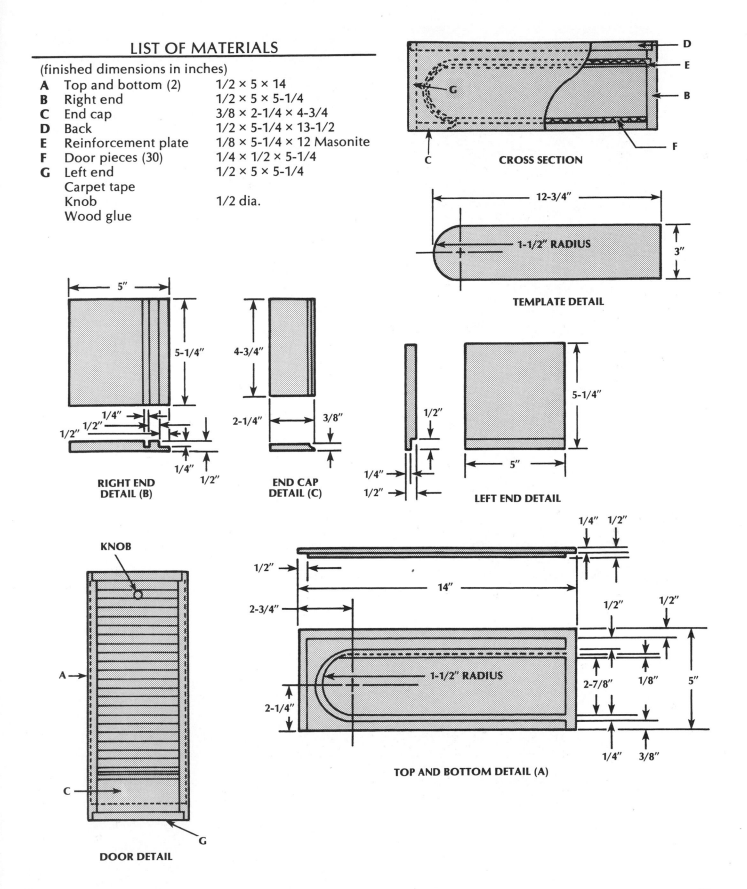

CROSS SECTION

TEMPLATE DETAIL

RIGHT END DETAIL (B)

END CAP DETAIL (C)

LEFT END DETAIL

TOP AND BOTTOM DETAIL (A)

KNOB

DOOR DETAIL

If you favor an Early American decor, this wall shelf is for you. Made of plywood and pine, it's the ideal showcase for those special family heirlooms.

1. Cut the pieces to size using the dimensions given. Use the patterns for cutting the tops of the sides (A) and the back (B).

2. Cut three dadoes in each side to accommodate the shelves (C, D). Rabbet the bottoms of the sides as shown.

3. Use fine sandpaper to smooth all cut edges.

4. Begin construction by attaching the facing strips (E) to the shelves with 1" brads.

5. Using 4d finishing nails, attach the shelves and sides to the back. For extra strength, wood glue can also be used.

6. Glue the decorative wood balls in place as shown.

7. Fill all nail holes with putty. Do any necessary finish sanding, then paint or stain as desired.

LIST OF MATERIALS

(finished dimensions in inches)

A	Sides (2)	1/2 × 8 × 30 plywood or pine
B	Back	1/2 × 23 × 32-1/2
C	Shelves (2)	1/2 × 7-1/4 × 23 plywood or pine
D	Shelves (2)	1/2 × 5 × 23 plywood or pine
E	Facing strips (4)	1/2 × 1/2 × 23 pine
	Decorative wood balls	1-1/8 dia.
	1" brads	
	4d finishing nails	
	Wood putty	
	Wood glue	

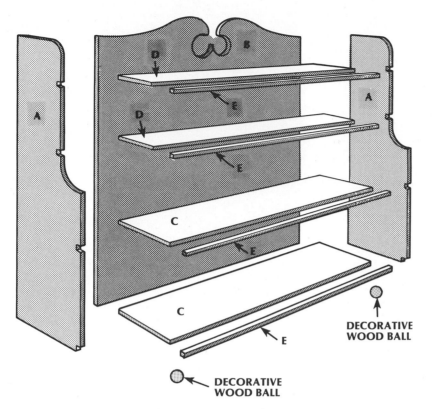

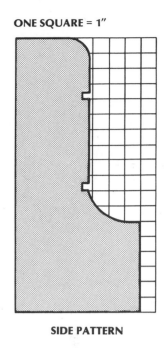

ONE SQUARE = 1"

SIDE PATTERN

DECORATIVE
WOOD BALL

DECORATIVE
WOOD BALL

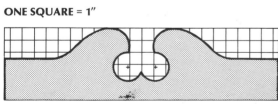

ONE SQUARE = 1"

BACK PATTERN

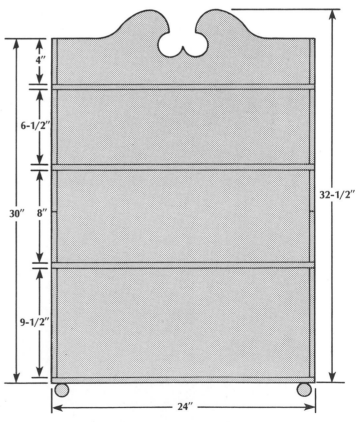

4"

6-1/2"

30"   8"

9-1/2"

32-1/2"

24"

FRONT DETAIL

Outdoor Projects

This section provides a wealth of outdoor projects, from a simple wood fence to a table and chair suitable for your patio, deck, or lawn. And not only will you gain a sense of accomplishment after completing them but you'll also end up with very practical, beautiful pieces.

Children love nothing better than to run, jump, climb, and swing, and this gym/play center is the perfect place for them to do all these things. In addition to pressure-treated lumber, you'll need four large barrels, four old tires, and a bicycle front fork and sleeve. Made to last for years, this project is truly a backyard "adventure center" for your children.

1. Cut all pieces of the gym/play center to size according to the dimensions given.

2. Measure in 32" from each end of the base pieces (C) and cut 3-1/2"-wide × 1-1/2"-deep dadoes.

3. Cut a 5-1/2"-wide × 1-3/4"-deep lap joint in one end of each of the uprights (A) and in both ends of each beam (B).

4. Assemble the frame, minus the tree house framing. Insert the end of the uprights opposite the lap joints into the dado in the base

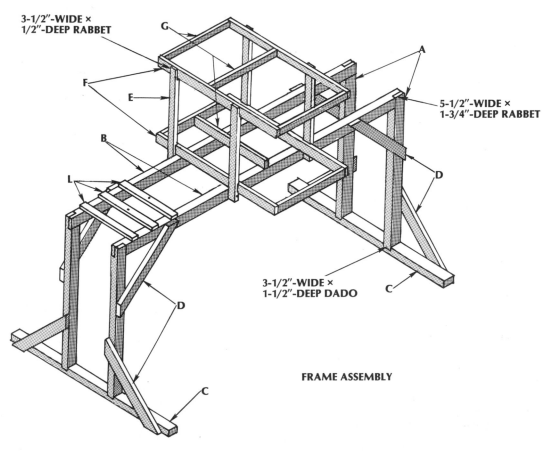

3-1/2"-WIDE × 1/2"-DEEP RABBET

5-1/2"-WIDE × 1-3/4"-DEEP RABBET

3-1/2"-WIDE × 1-1/2"-DEEP DADO

FRAME ASSEMBLY

pieces. Nail through the base into the upright with 16d galvanized nails. Brace the uprights temporarily to hold them in position while attaching the rest of the frame. NOTE: To reinforce the joints of the play center, use wood glue during all phases of assembly.

5. With the uprights vertical, have an assistant position the lap joints of the beams in the lap joints of the uprights. Temporarily clamp the beams in place. Drill two 5/16"-diameter holes through each lap joint and install carriage bolts with washers and nuts.

6. Bevel the ends of the diagonal braces (D). Temporarily clamp the braces in position on the uprights and bases and uprights and beams. Drill 1/4"-diameter holes and install 1/4" × 4" lag screws and washers.

7. Drill a 1/2"-diameter hole centered in the face of two of the steps (L). Beginning with the step that was not drilled, attach all three steps to the beams with 16d galvanized nails.

8. Cut a 3-1/2"-wide × 1/2"-deep rabbet in one end of each tree house stud (E). Cut 3-1/2"-wide × 1/2"-deep dadoes in the opposite ends, but set them in 5-1/2" from the end. These will be used to attach the long frame pieces (F) later.

9. Temporarily clamp the tree house studs to the beams. Drill a 3/8"-diameter hole through the edge of each stud and through the beams. Attach the studs to the beams with 3/8" × 7" carriage bolts, washers, and nuts.

10. Attach the long frames of the tree house to the short frames (G) with 5/16" × 1-3/4" carriage bolts. Attach the siding (K) with 6d galvanized nails.

11. Install the tree house flooring slats, using 6d galvanized nails to nail through the slats and into the long frames. Leave a 1/2" gap between slats.

12. Attach the fiberglass roof with 1"-long roofing nails. If using corrugated fiberglass, buy and cut two

LIST OF MATERIALS

(finished dimensions in inches)

A	Uprights (4)	3-1/2 × 5-1/2 × 78
B	Beams (2)	3-1/2 × 5-1/2 × 168
C	Base pieces (2)	3-1/2 × 5-1/2 × 96
D	Diagonal braces (8)	1-1/2 × 3-1/2 × 46
E	Tree house studs (4)	1-1/2 × 3-1/2 × 48
F	Tree house long frame pieces (4)	1-1/2 × 3-1/2 × 72
G	Tree house short frames (6)	1-1/2 × 3-1/2 × 41
H	Firefighter's pole brace	3/4 × 5-1/2 × 41
J	Flooring slats (8)	3/4 × 5-1/2 × 44
K	Tree house siding (10)	3/4 × 5-1/2 × 42-1/2
L	Steps (3)	1-1/2 × 3-1/2 × 32
M	Barrel spin supports (3)	1-1/2 × 3-1/2 × 32
N	Center barrel supports (2)	1-1/2 × 9-1/4 × 32
P	Barrel supports (5)	1-1/2 × 9-1/4 × 32
Q	Tree house barrel supports (2)	1-1/2 × 3-1/2 × 32
R	Trapeze bar	1-1/2 dia. × 14
S	Barrel support braces (2)	1-1/2 × 3-1/2 × 12-3/4
T	Swing seat	1-1/2 × 9-1/4 × 44
U	Closures (2)	1 × 1-1/2 × 46
	Carriage bolts, washers, and nuts	5/16 × 3-1/2
	Carriage bolts, washers, and nuts	5/16 × 1-3/4
	Carriage bolts, washers, and nuts	3/8 × 7
	Lag screws and washers	1/4 × 2
	Lag screws and washers	1/4 × 4
	Brass flathead wood screws	#10 × 2
	Panhead wood screws	#16 × 1
	Tree house roof	1/8 × 46 × 48 fiberglass
	Steel plates (2)	1/8 × 3 × 4
	Galvanized pipe and cap	2 dia. × 144
	Rope	1/2 dia.
	Band irons (3)	1/8 × 1 × 40
	Swing set chain	16 lineal feet
	6d galvanized nails	
	16d galvanized nails	
	Roofing nails	
	Tires (4)	
	Bicycle front fork and sleeve	
	Barrels (4)	
	Hose or insulation pipe	
	Sand	
	Waterproof wood glue	

redwood closures (U) to the corrugated shape to fit under the edge of the roof.

13. Drill a 2"-diameter hole centered in the face of the firefighter's pole brace (H). Using a 2"-diameter × 12-foot-long galvanized pipe as the firefighter's pole, slide it through the hole in the brace. Nail the brace between the upper long frames to support the pole.

14. Set the pole in the center of an old tire, and plant the pole approximately one foot into the ground. Fill the inside of the tire with sand to provide a soft landing area for children sliding down the pole.

15. Cut out both ends of three of the barrels, and cut out one end of the remaining barrel. Coat the barrels inside and out with exterior polyurethane.

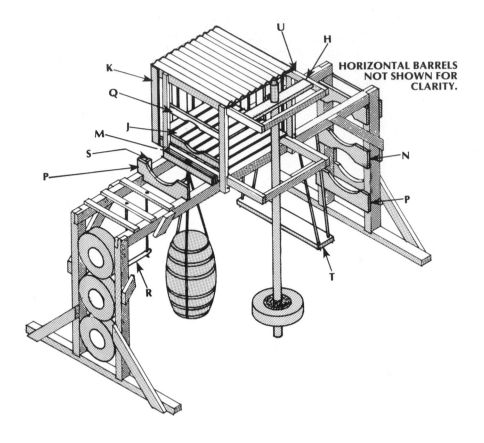

HORIZONTAL BARRELS
NOT SHOWN FOR
CLARITY.

16. Drill drainage holes in the remaining barrel bottom. Fasten the hoops to three of the barrels with #16 × 1″ panhead wood screws to keep them from loosening due to barrel shrinkage. Do not fasten the hoops to any of the barrels that have both ends cut out; they are needed as templates for the barrel supports (P).

17. The barrel spin hangs and turns on an axis consisting of a bicycle front fork and sleeve; you should be able to salvage these parts from an old bike. Cut off the pieces with a hacksaw as shown in the drawings.

18. Weld two 1/8″ × 3″ × 4″ steel plates to the sleeve as shown.

19. Weld or screw three 1/8″ × 1″ × 40″ band irons to the hoops around the barrel with a bottom. The irons must be perpendicular to the hoops, evenly spaced around the barrel, and extend beyond the top of the open end.

20. Drill a 3/8″-diameter hole in the end of each band iron to hook a chain. Then drill a 3/8″-diameter

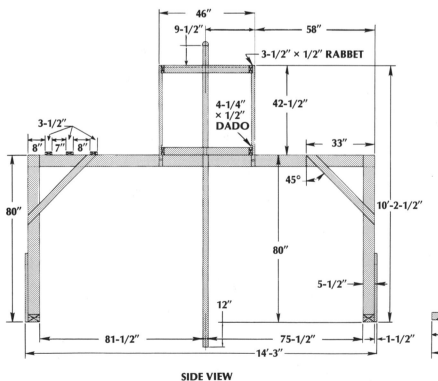

SIDE VIEW

END VIEW

FRAME AND FIREMAN'S POLE LAYOUT

hole through the bottom of the front fork as shown. A bolt is inserted in this hole to attach the chains leading to the barrel.

21. Place the modified bicycle front fork and sleeve between the barrel spin supports (M). Glue and nail the supports together.

22. Fasten the steel plates to the barrel spin supports with #10 × 2" flathead wood screws. Set the supports crossways on top of the beams and secure with 16d galvanized nails.

23. Insert a 3/8"-diameter bolt through the hole in the front fork, through the link of the three chains, and out the hole in the front fork. Tighten a nut and washer on the end of the bolt.

24. Before hooking the chains to the barrel, slip them through rubber hose or insulation pipe for pro-

tection. Then hook the chains to the band irons extending from the barrel.

25. The other barrels are attached horizontally for children to crawl through. Take the hoop not fastened to a barrel and use it as a template to draw the diameter on the barrel supports. Cut them to shape on a bandsaw. Replace the hoop on the barrel and fasten with #16 × 1" panhead wood screws as with the other hoops in step 16.

26. Attach two of the barrels at one end of the play center by first temporarily clamping the lower barrel supports in position. Drill 1/4"-diameter holes through the supports, and attach the supports to the uprights with 1/4" × 4" lag screws and washers.

27. Set the lower barrel in place, clamp a center barrel support (N)

in place, and drill a 1/4"-diameter hole. Attach the lower barrel with 1/4" × 4" lag screws. Repeat for the upper barrel.

28. Fasten the barrels to the supports with #10 × 2" flathead wood screws from inside the barrels. Attach the barrel leading into the tree house in the same manner.

29. Turn the trapeze bar (R) on a lathe. Drill a 1/2"-diameter hole in each end of the bar, then hang it from the steps with 1/2"-diameter rope (using the holes that were drilled in step 7).

30. Drill two 1/2"-diameter holes at each end of the swing seat (T). Drill matching holes in the beam overhead, then hang the swing with 1/2"-diameter rope.

31. At the end of the play center opposite the barrels, attach the three remaining tires with 1/4" × 2"

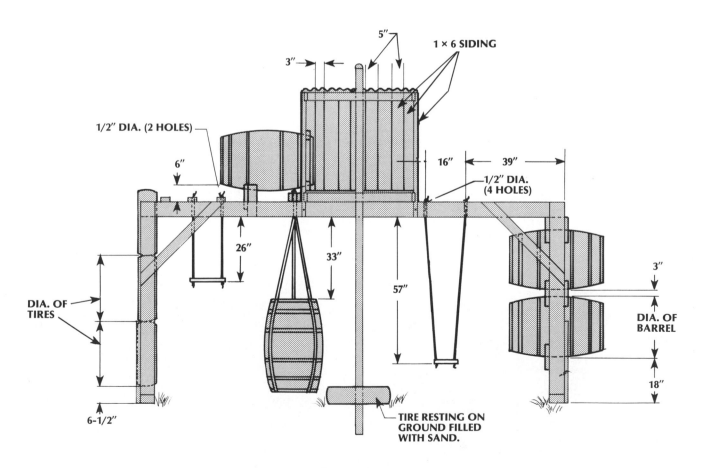

FRONT LAYOUT

lag screws. Drive the screws into the uprights as shown, then bolt the tires together to keep them from twisting.

32. Finally, drill a drainage hole in the bottom of each tire.

33. Inspect the play gym. Make sure *all* exposed edges are rounded or beveled, all splinters are removed, all metal edges are covered, and no nails are protruding.

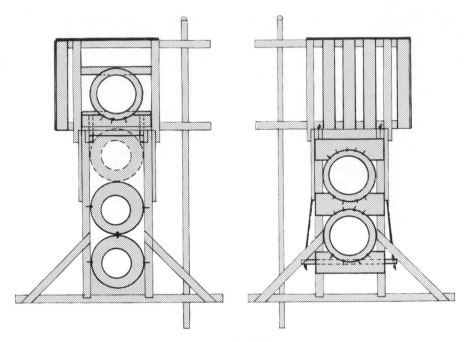

SIDE LAYOUTS

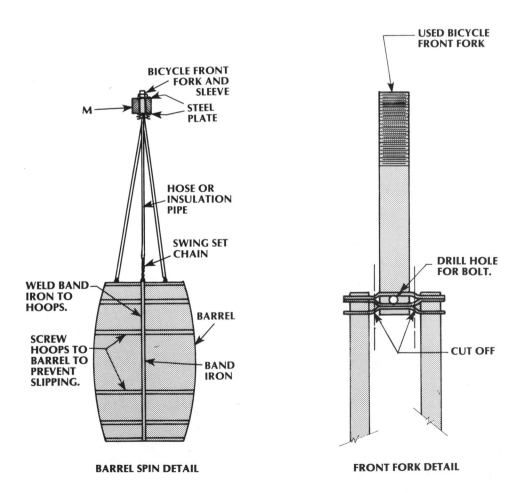

BARREL SPIN DETAIL

FRONT FORK DETAIL

The measurements for this planter box are based on a standard kitchen trash can, which is used as a liner for indoor/outdoor use. Western red cedar was used in this example, but any weather-resistant wood will work well. Be sure to provide adequate drainage; a totally sealed planter will eventually cause the plant roots to rot and die.

1. Cut the pieces of the planter to size according to the dimensions given. Bevel the top and bottom of the sides (A) and the edges of the bottom (C).
2. With the saw table tilted at 44-3/4° and the miter gauge at 85°, cut the compound miter joints in the sides.
3. Change the miter gauge setting to 45° and return the table to 90°; then cut the miters in the top pieces (B).
4. Cut a 7/8"-wide × 1/2"-deep groove in the underside of the top pieces.
5. Assemble the top pieces with 8d galvanized finishing nails.
6. Assemble the sides with nails. Slide the bottom into place, and secure it by nailing.
7. Drill four holes in the bottom for drainage.
8. The top can either be nailed or glued in place, or left loose so that it can be easily removed for maintenance.
9. If finish is desired, use a good outdoor finish such as spar varnish or exterior polyurethane.

LIST OF MATERIALS

(finished dimensions in inches)

A	Sides (4)	3/4 × 11-1/2 × 16-1/4
B	Top pieces (4)	3/4 × 2 × 13-1/2
C	Bottom	3/4 × 7-5/8 × 7-5/8

#8 galvanized finishing nails
Water-resistant wood glue

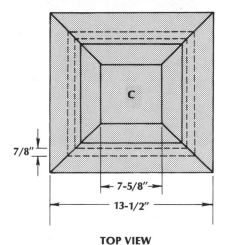

TOP VIEW

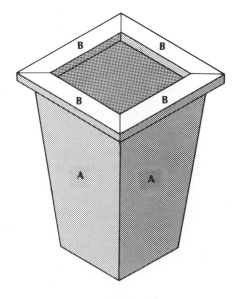

CONSTRUCTION DETAIL

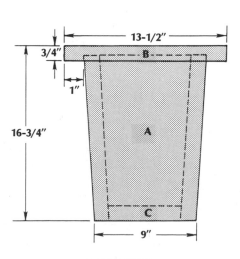

FRONT VIEW

SANDBOX

This sandbox design features a translucent roof that sheds rain and shields your children from the sun. Shelves allow toys to be stored out of the sand, and the bench offers comfortable seating. Building the sandbox with pressure-treated lumber and installing an aluminum floor make this a project that will last for years to come.

1. After cutting all the pieces to size, lay out and mark the 45° angles on the shelf supports (M) and seat supports (P). Cut these angles on a bandsaw or table saw with a miter gauge.

2. Drill 1/4"-diameter holes in the roof frame sides (A), posts (D, E, F), and sides (G) for carriage bolts. To prevent splintering, drill the holes partially through the pieces until the bit point breaks though, then turn the pieces over and complete the holes.

3. Predrill the holes needed for the #10 × 1-1/2" flathead wood screws that will be used to assemble the sandbox.

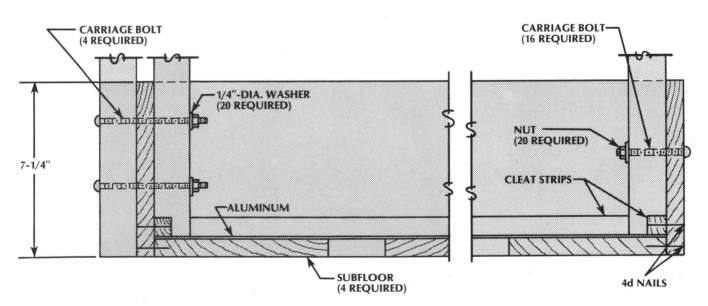

FLOORING DETAIL

LIST OF MATERIALS

(finished dimensions in inches)

A	Roof frame sides (2)	3/4 × 2 × 45-1/2
B	Roof frame cross members (4)	3/4 × 2 × 36
C	Roof	37-1/2 × 45-1/2 corrugated fiberglass
D	Rear shelf posts (2)	1-1/2 × 1-1/2 × 45-1/2
E	Front shelf posts (2)	1-1/2 × 1-1/2 × 44-3/4
F	Seat posts (2)	1-1/2 × 1-1/2 × 48
G	Sides (4)	3/4 × 7-1/4 × 36-3/4
H	Cleat strips (4)	3/4 × 3/4 × 33
J	Floor	0.04-ga. × 36 × 36 aluminum
K	Shelf rails (3)	3/4 × 1-1/2 × 33
L	Shelves (3)	3/4 × 7-1/4 × 33
M	Shelf supports (6)	3/4 × 3-1/2 × 6
N	Seat	3/4 × 7-1/4 × 33
P	Seat supports (2)	3/4 × 4 × 6-3/4
Q	Subflooring (4)	3/4 × 7-1/4 × 36
	Carriage bolts	1/4-20 × 2-1/2
	Carriage bolts	1/4-20 × 4-1/2
	Brass flathead wood screws	#10 × 1-1/2
	Panhead sheet metal screws	#6 × 1/2
	6d finishing nails	
	Nuts and washers	
	Water-resistant wood glue	

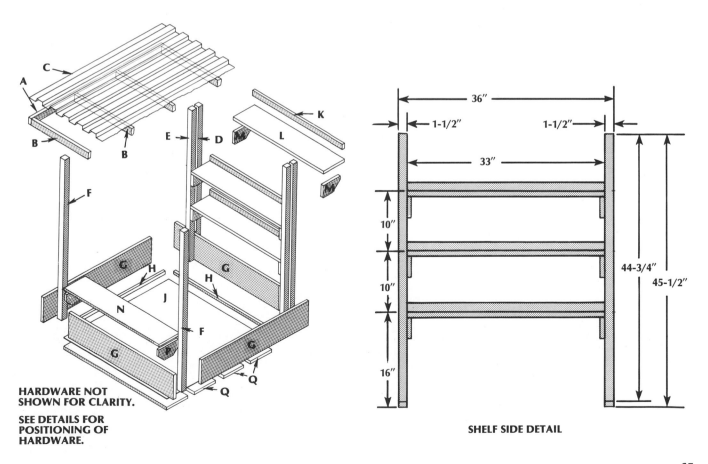

HARDWARE NOT
SHOWN FOR CLARITY.

SEE DETAILS FOR
POSITIONING OF
HARDWARE.

SHELF SIDE DETAIL

4. Sand all the pieces thoroughly with a belt sander or orbital sander. This is important to prevent your children from getting splinters while playing.

5. Assemble the base by attaching the sides to form a box. Secure the sides with wood screws and glue. Then add the subflooring (Q), using 6d finishing nails and glue. Set the base aside.

6. Attach the shelves (L) and seat (N) to their supports (M, P) with wood screws. Attach the shelves to the shelf posts with wood screws, then attach the seat to the seat posts with #20 × 2-1/2 carriage bolts. Do not glue the shelves or seat to their posts. Set these assemblies aside.

7. Construct the roof frame by assembling the sides and cross members (B) with wood screws and glue.

8. If desired, stain or finish all wooden pieces and assemblies with a good outdoor finish, such as polyurethane or spar varnish. Do not continue assembly until the finish has completely dried.

9. Attach the roof (C) to the roof frame with #6 panhead sheet metal screws.

10. Set the floor (J) in place over the subflooring. Secure it by nailing and gluing cleat strips (H) to the sides.

11. Attach the shelf and post assembly and the seat and post assembly to the base with #20 × 4-1/2 carriage bolts. Finally, bolt the roof assembly to the posts.

12. Inspect the sandbox. Make sure *all* exposed edges are rounded or beveled, all splinters are removed, all metal edges are covered, and no nails are protruding.

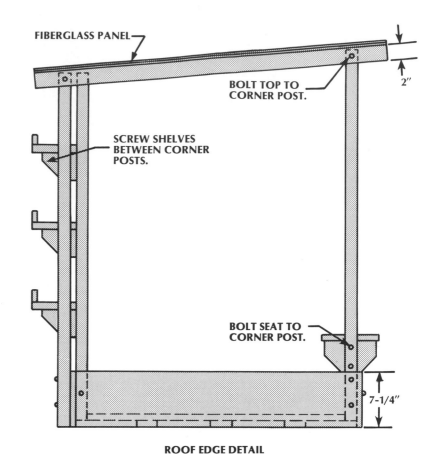

ROOF EDGE DETAIL

BASE ASSEMBLY

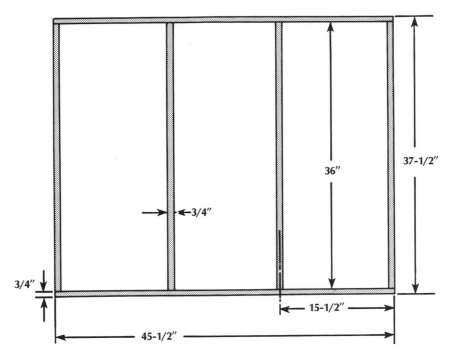

ROOF FRAME DETAIL

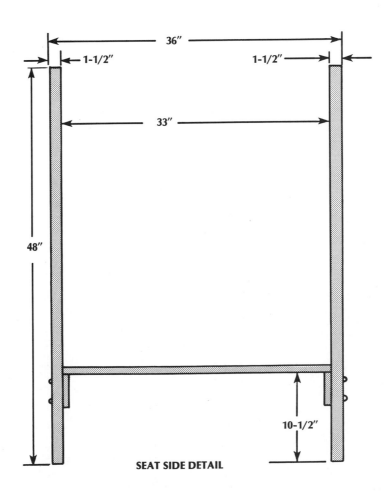

SEAT SIDE DETAIL

Here's an item that makes barbecuing more fun and gardening easier—a patio cart. Although it takes up less than 4-1/2 square feet of floor space, its shelves hold a great deal.

1. Cut all pieces to size according to the dimensions provided.

2. Cut 1/2"-wide grooves 1/4" deep into the shelf front and rear (C) and the shelf sides (D, E). The grooves in the sides should be stop grooves.

3. Assemble the shelf bottoms (F, G) and sides with 6d finishing nails. Set the nails and fill the holes with wood putty.

4. Drill 3/4"-diameter holes in the diagonals (A) to accommodate the axles (H) and handle (K).

5. Cut lap joints in the diagonals and uprights (B) as shown, then assemble them with 6d finishing nails and glue.

6. Drill 1/4"-diameter wheel pin holes in the ends of the axles.

7. Cut out the wheels (M) on a bandsaw or jigsaw. Sand them to a smooth contour, then drill a 3/4"-diameter axle hole in each one.

8. Finish all pieces before continuing with the remainder of the assembly.

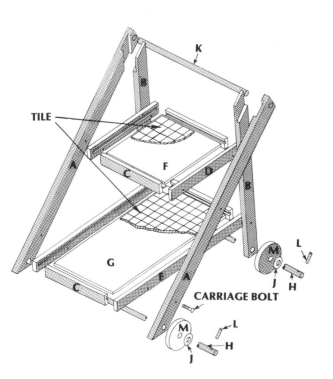

LIST OF MATERIALS

(finished dimensions in inches)

A	Diagonals (2)	1-1/2 × 2 × 46-1/2
B	Uprights (2)	1-1/2 × 2 × 31-3/4
C	Shelf front and rear (4)	3/4 × 2 × 13-1/2
D	Shelf sides (2)	3/4 × 2 × 16-1/2
E	Shelf sides (2)	3/4 × 2 × 31-3/8
F	Shelf bottom	1/2 × 14 × 15-1/2
G	Shelf bottom	1/2 × 14 × 30-3/8
H	Axles (2)	3/4 dia. × 20-1/2
J	Spacers (8)	2 dia. × 1/16
K	Handle	3/4 dia. × 17-1/2
L	Wheel pins (4)	1/4 dia. × 17-1/2
M	Wheels (4)	5 dia. × 3/4
	Carriage bolts and washers	1/4 × 2-1/2
	Ceramic tile	
	6d finishing nails	
	Grout	
	Wood putty	
	Water-resistant wood glue	

9. Using spacers (J) and wheel pins (L), assemble the axles and wheels to the frame. Attach the handle to the frame with glue.

10. Clamp the assembled shelves to the frame. Drill 1/4"-diameter bolt holes in the frame and shelves for final assembly.

11. Clean the shelf surfaces thoroughly. Apply a waterproof ceramic adhesive evenly on the shelves with a trowel, and press the tile into place.

12. Spread grout into the tile grooves with a squeegee. Wipe away the excess with a clean squeegee, then wash the remaining grout from the face of the tile with a damp sponge. When the tile has set, use a clean, dry cloth for the final cleaning.

13. Attach the shelves to the frame with carriage bolts to complete the cart.

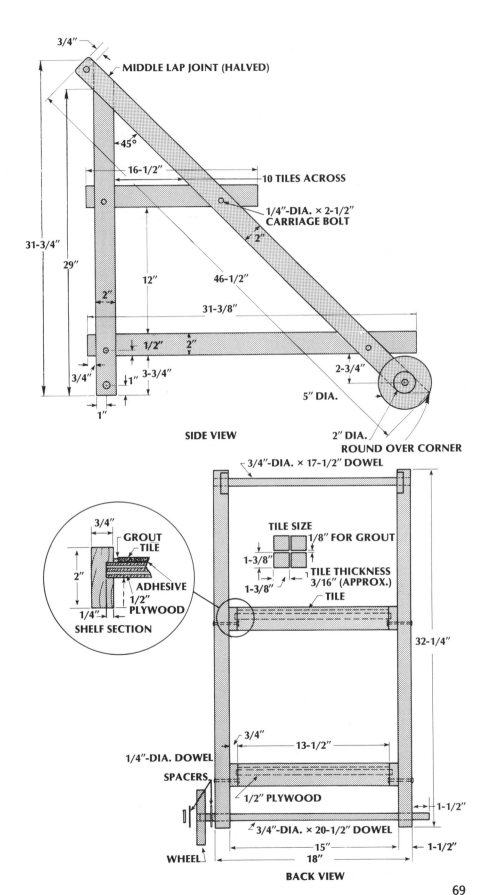

SIDE VIEW

SHELF SECTION

BACK VIEW

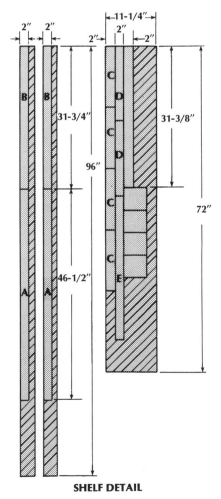

SHELF DETAIL

PICNIC TABLE/BENCH

This unique design enables everyone to sit on the same side, making it very handy for serving your guests. It also folds into a bench when not needed as a table.

1. Start construction by cutting all the pieces to size. Note that the ends of the legs (B, C) and one end of the leg braces (D) are cut at a 5° angle.

2. Cut a dado joint in the back legs to accommodate the back brace (E).

3. Drill pivot holes in the back legs and pivot blocks (F) as shown. Do not drill the stop pinholes at this time; they will be drilled later for accurate positioning and alignment.

4. Drill the bolt holes in each piece as indicated in the patterns. Sand all the pieces to guard against splinters. The table is ready for assembly.

5. Assemble the front and back legs to the leg braces using bolts, washers, and nuts.

6. Assemble the back brace to the back legs with wood screws. Then attach the seat pieces (A) to the leg braces with wood screws and the pivot blocks to the outside of the back legs with bolts, washers, and nuts.

7. Assemble the top/backrest pieces (A) to the pivot blocks with wood screws.

8. To drill the stop pinholes, clamp the tabletop in its level position and drill a hole through both the pivot block and back leg on both ends of the table.

9. Tilt the tabletop to the backrest position and clamp again. Now drill another hole through the pivot blocks. (Be sure to drill from the inside and through the previously drilled stop pinhole in the legs.) Use eye bolts with two washers and wing nuts as the stop pins.

10. For redwood, cedar, or pressure-treated wood, no finish is necessary. If other lumber is used, finish the table with spar varnish, polyurethane, or other suitable outdoor finish.

LIST OF MATERIALS
(finished dimensions in inches)

A	Top/backrest and seat (5)	1-1/2 × 5-1/2 × 60
B	Back legs (2)	1-1/2 × 3-1/2 × 29-1/2
C	Front legs (2)	1-1/2 × 3-1/2 × 17-1/2
D	Leg braces (2)	1-1/2 × 3-1/2 × 26
E	Back brace	1-1/2 × 3-1/2 × 48-1/2
F	Pivot blocks (2)	1-1/2 × 7-1/4 × 16
	Brass flathead wood screws	#12 × 3
	Bolts and eye bolts	5/16 × 3
	Washers, nuts, and wing nuts	

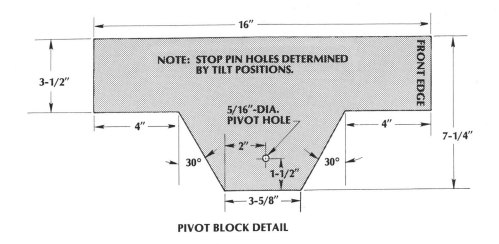

NOTE: STOP PIN HOLES DETERMINED BY TILT POSITIONS.

16"

3-1/2"

FRONT EDGE

4"

5/16"-DIA. PIVOT HOLE

2"

30°

1-1/2"

30°

4"

7-1/4"

3-5/8"

PIVOT BLOCK DETAIL

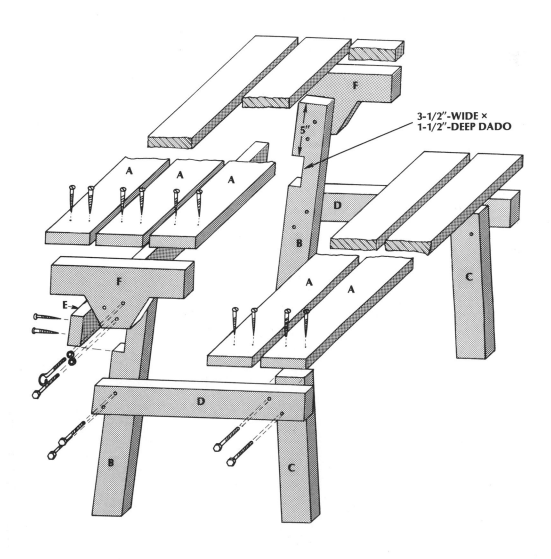

5"

3-1/2"-WIDE × 1-1/2"-DEEP DADO

A A A

F

D

B

E

F

A A

C

D

B

C

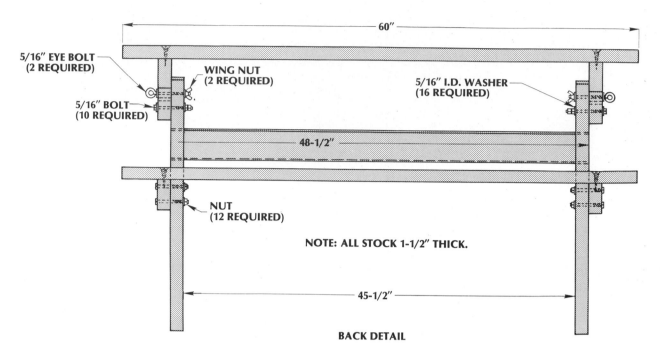

5/16" EYE BOLT
(2 REQUIRED)

WING NUT
(2 REQUIRED)

5/16" I.D. WASHER
(16 REQUIRED)

5/16" BOLT
(10 REQUIRED)

60"

48-1/2"

NUT
(12 REQUIRED)

NOTE: ALL STOCK 1-1/2" THICK.

45-1/2"

BACK DETAIL

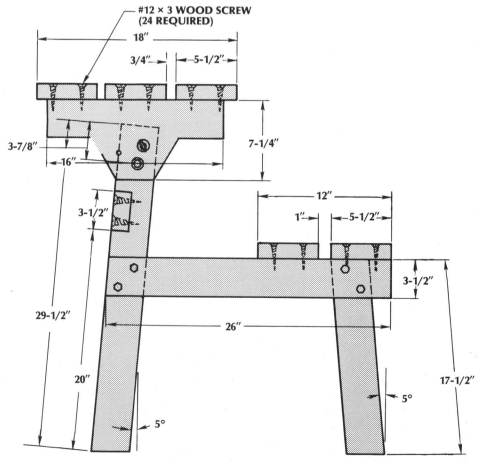

#12 × 3 WOOD SCREW
(24 REQUIRED)

18"

3/4"   5-1/2"

7-1/4"

3-7/8"

16"

12"

1"   5-1/2"

3-1/2"

3-1/2"

29-1/2"

26"

20"

17-1/2"

5°

5°

SIDE DETAIL

BIRDHOUSE

Why not introduce the birds in your neighborhood to apartment-style living with this unique birdhouse? It's designed to house four families in separate compartments.

1. Cut all of the pieces to size according to the dimensions provided.

2. Cut approximately 2-1/2"-diameter entrance holes in the front pieces (E, F). Drill 1/2"-diameter holes below the entrance holes to accommodate the perches.

3. Construct the center section by nailing the partition (G) to the front and back at the midpoint between the top and bottom of the birdhouse.

4. Glue and nail the sides (C) in place.

5. Nail the floor pieces (D) to the center section so that it is centered evenly.

6. Attach the side partitions (H) by nailing all of the pieces together.

7. Finally, bevel the roof pieces (A, B) at 45° angles and nail them in place.

8. Finish the birdhouse as desired, then add 1/2"-diameter dowels to serve as the perches.

LIST OF MATERIALS

(finished dimensions in inches)

A	Center roof pieces (2)	3/4 × 5-1/2 × 13-3/4
B	Side roof pieces (4)	3/4 × 5-1/2 × 13-3/4
C	Sides (2)	3/4 × 5-1/2 × 11
D	Floor pieces (2)	3/4 × 5-1/2 × 18
E	Front and back center pieces (2)	3/4 × 5-1/2 × 16
F	Front and back side pieces (4)	3/4 × 5-1/2 × 11
G	Center partition	3/4 × 5-1/2 × ~~11~~ 9 1/2
H	Side partitions ~~(4)~~ 2 -	3/4 × 5-1/2 × 9-1/2
	Dowels (4)	1/2 dia. × 3-1/2
	Nails	
	Water-resistant wood glue	

2- 3/4 x 7 x 9 1/2

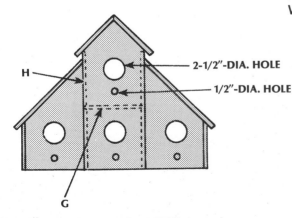

H
G
2-1/2"-DIA. HOLE
1/2"-DIA. HOLE

CONSTRUCTION DETAIL

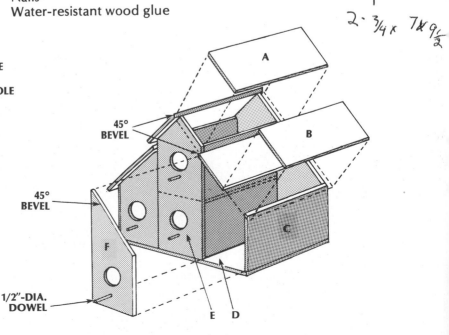

A
B
45° BEVEL
45° BEVEL
F
E D
1/2"-DIA. DOWEL

REDWOOD PLANTER

This spacious redwood planter is perfect for large plants or an arrangement of flowers. It's easy to build and can be used both indoors and out.

1. Start with five 8' boards (three 2 × 6s and two 1 × 8s) and three feet of 1/2"-diameter dowel rod. Cut all the pieces to size by following the diagram.

2. Cut 45° miters on both ends of the top frame pieces and the leg tops (B). Cut 45° miters on one end of each leg (A) as well.

3. Drill 1/2"-diameter dowel holes 1-1/8" deep into the mitered ends of the top frame pieces.

4. Drill twelve 1/2"-diameter holes in the bottom pieces (E) for proper drainage.

5. Attach the cleat strips (G, H) to the front and side panels (C, D) with 4d finishing nails. Attach the front panels to the side panels, also with 4d finishing nails.

6. Attach the legs to the leg tops with 4d finishing nails or dowels and glue. Attach the leg assembly to the box with #8 × 1-1/2" flathead wood screws.

7. Use 2" dowels and glue to put the top frame pieces together. Attach the top frame (J) to the top of the box with 8d finishing nails.

8. Countersink all nails; fill the holes with redwood-tinted wood putty.

9. Finish the planter with a good outdoor finish, or let the redwood weather naturally.

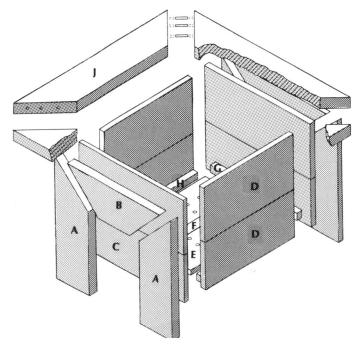

LIST OF MATERIALS

(finished dimensions in inches)

A	Legs (4)	1-1/2 × 5-1/2 × 18
B	Leg tops (2)	1-1/2 × 5-1/2 × 20
C	Front pieces (4)	3/4 × 7-1/4 × 17-1/2
D	Side pieces (4)	3/4 × 7-1/4 × 16
E	Bottom pieces (2)	3/4 × 7-1/4 × 15-7/8
F	Bottom (center)	3/4 × 1-7/16 × 15-7/8
G	Cleat strips (2)	3/4 × 1 × 14-1/2
H	Cleat strips (2)	3/4 × 1 × 16
J	Top frame (4)	1-1/2 × 5-1/2 × 27
	Dowels (12)	1/2 dia. × 2
	Brass flathead wood screws	#8 × 1-1/2
	4d finishing nails	
	8d finishing nails	
	Wood putty	
	Water-resistant wood glue	

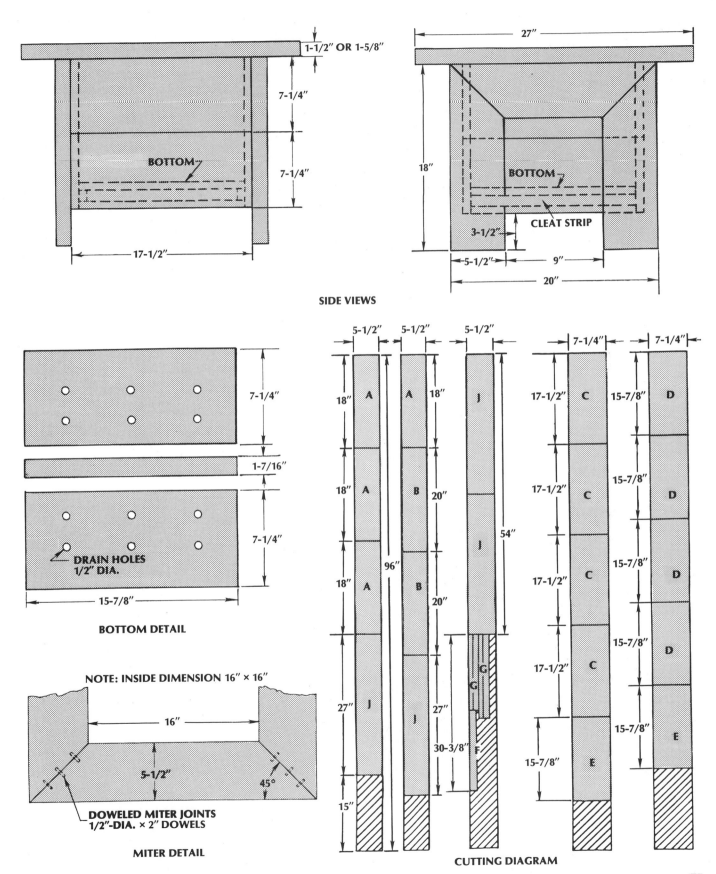

1-1/2" OR 1-5/8"

7-1/4"

7-1/4"

BOTTOM

17-1/2"

27"

18"

BOTTOM

CLEAT STRIP

3-1/2"

5-1/2"

9"

20"

SIDE VIEWS

7-1/4"

1-7/16"

7-1/4"

DRAIN HOLES
1/2" DIA.

15-7/8"

BOTTOM DETAIL

NOTE: INSIDE DIMENSION 16" × 16"

16"

5-1/2"

45°

DOWELED MITER JOINTS
1/2"-DIA. × 2" DOWELS

MITER DETAIL

5-1/2"   5-1/2"   5-1/2"   7-1/4"   7-1/4"

18"   A   A   18"   J   17-1/2"   C   15-7/8"   D

18"   A   B   20"   17-1/2"   C   15-7/8"   D

96"   J   54"

18"   A   B   20"   17-1/2"   C   15-7/8"   D

G

27"   J   J   27"   G   17-1/2"   C   15-7/8"   D

30-3/8"   F

17-1/2"   C   15-7/8"   E

15"   15-7/8"   E

CUTTING DIAGRAM

LAWN CHAIR

This comfortable outdoor chair can be easily adapted into a lounge chair or love seat. By changing a few more dimensions, you can have a bench/sofa; however, the seat slats must be increased to 1-1/8" thickness. In any event, you'll find that the chair can be built at a fraction of retail prices.

1. Cut the stock to size according to the dimensions given. Use the patterns provided to cut the contoured pieces. Make any size adjustments now if you are building a variation of the chair.

2. Cut a 1/2" radius on the edges of the seat supports (B). If a router is used, a smaller radius is acceptable.

3. Using 3/8"-diameter dowels and glue, assemble the seat supports and back supports (A) as shown.

4. With a bandsaw or jigsaw, cut the seat and back assembly to the correct shape, then sand for final assembly.

5. Using 3/8"-diameter dowels and glue, attach the legs (C, D) to the seat and back assembly.

6. The spreaders (E) are also attached with dowels and glue. Use extra care at this stage to ensure squareness.

7. Finally, secure the slats (F) with #8 × 1-1/4" wood screws. Use a 1/2" wood block to space the slats parallel and at 1/2" intervals. Finish as desired.

LIST OF MATERIALS

(finished dimensions in inches)

A	Back supports (2)	3/4 × 6 × 28
B	Seat supports (2)	3/4 × 6 × 21
C	Front legs (2)	3/4 × 3-1/2 × 14
D	Back legs (2)	3/4 × 3-1/2 × 12
E	Spreaders (2)	3/4 × 3 × 18
F	Slats (20)	3/4 × 2-1/4 × 22
	Dowels (20)	3/8 dia. × 1-1/2
	Brass flathead wood screws	#8 × 1-1/4
	Water-resistant wood glue	

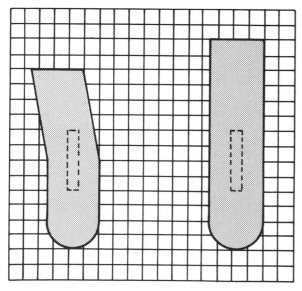

BACK LEG PATTERNS

ONE SQUARE = 1"

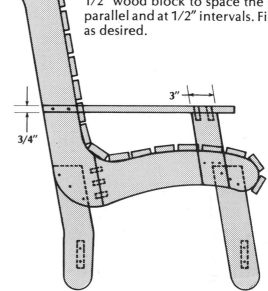

3"

3/4"

SIDE VIEW WITH OPTIONAL ARM

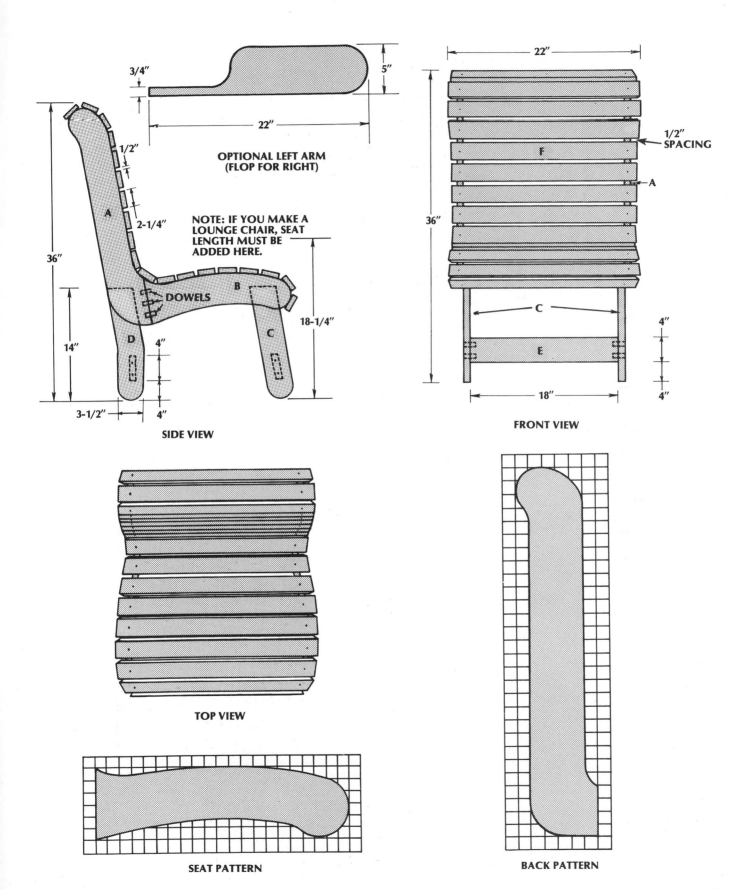

3/4"

5"

22"

**OPTIONAL LEFT ARM
(FLOP FOR RIGHT)**

22"

1/2"

2-1/4"

**NOTE: IF YOU MAKE A
LOUNGE CHAIR, SEAT
LENGTH MUST BE
ADDED HERE.**

36"

A

B

DOWELS

D

C

14"

4"

18-1/4"

3-1/2"

4"

SIDE VIEW

22"

**1/2"
SPACING**

F

A

36"

C

E

4"

18"

4"

FRONT VIEW

TOP VIEW

SEAT PATTERN

BACK PATTERN

LAWN TABLE

Here is an end table to complement your wooden lawn chairs. And with only minor variations in the length of the top slats, it can be easily transformed into an outdoor coffee table. By extending the height of the legs, it becomes a handy serving table. You're limited only by your imagination.

1. Cut all of the pieces to size according to the dimensions given.

2. Miter the ends of the side rails (B), then cut grooves in the mitered edges for inserting the splines (D) as shown in the detail drawing. The grooves should be perpendicular to the mitered edge and slightly more than half as deep as the width of the spline.

3. Dry-assemble the side rails. When satisfied with the fit, glue, clamp, and insert the splines, being careful to maintain squareness.

4. Use a dado blade to cut the half lap joints on the tops of the legs (C).

5. Clamp the legs to the side rails, then attach with dowels and glue. Again, be sure to maintain squareness.

6. Clamp, glue, and dowel the top slats (A) to the side rails. Use a 1/2" spacer block to keep the slats parallel and the spacing uniform.

7. Although outdoor woods require no additional finish, spar varnish or an exterior polyurethane make attractive natural finishes.

1/2" SPACING   A   D

5/8"

B

16"

C   C

1-1/2"

20-1/2"

FRONT VIEW

LIST OF MATERIALS
(finished dimensions in inches)

A	Top slats (7)	5/8 × 2-1/2 × 20-1/2
B	Side rails (4)	3/4 × 2 × 20-1/2
C	Legs (4)	1-1/2 × 1-1/2 × 15-3/8
D	Splines (4)	1/8 × 3/4 × 2
	Dowels	3/8 dia. × 1-1/2
	Water-resistant wood glue	

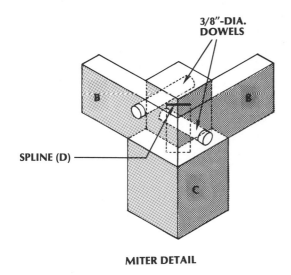

3/8"-DIA. DOWELS

SPLINE (D)

MITER DETAIL

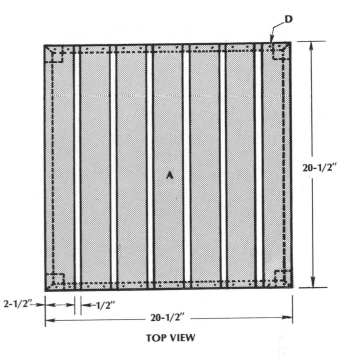

D

A

20-1/2"

2-1/2" 1/2" 20-1/2"

TOP VIEW

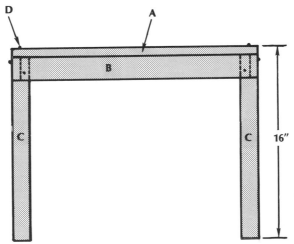

D

A

B

C

C

16"

SIDE VIEW

Nothing accents a home's exterior better than a wood fence. It also provides a degree of privacy as well as a means of keeping children and/or pets within your property. There are many different fence styles to choose from: dog ear, sawtooth, board-on-board, post-and-rail, stockade, several types of picket, or even a unique design of your own.

When gathering materials, keep in mind that pressure-treated lumber is best, especially for underground posts. It offers superior decay resistance and can last up to 50 years. Use only high-quality galvanized aluminum alloy or stainless steel nails and other fasteners. Any other metal will corrode and stain the wood with hard-to-remove streaks. When figuring concrete, a standard 90-pound bag makes approximately 2/3 cubic foot—or one bag per hole.

Before beginning, make a rough drawing of the area to be fenced with all measurements, including the gates. Four feet is the standard height, but fences can range from three to eight feet high; consult your local building codes. Lumber is sold in multiples of two feet, so if you need 4-1/2-foot boards it would be wise to cut four boards out of an 18-footer with no waste rather than two boards from a 10-footer with scrap left over. Add 10 percent to your totals to allow for waste and errors.

1. The first step in construction is to set the posts, a very important step if the fence is to be straight. Generally, a fence three to six feet high requires 4 × 4 posts set in holes 24" deep. In the north, 36" holes are recommended. If your fence is seven or eight feet high, add 12" to the post hole depth. All corner and gate posts should be set an extra 12" deep as well, because they need greater support.

2. In the bottom of the hole, set a base stone or a 4" layer of sand or gravel. Set the post in the hole, add concrete to within 3" of the top of the hole, and top off with 4" of soil.

NOTE: Tamped dirt can be used instead of concrete for fences no higher than four feet, but concrete is still the best anchor.

3. The most effective method of setting posts is the corner post method. Set the corner or end posts first, positioning them with their faces parallel. Plumb with a level and set the posts permanently. Stretch twine between the corner posts, set and align the posts in between, plumb the posts on two sides as you go, and permanently set the remaining posts.

4. The next step is to add rails and siding. If the pickets are to be placed with a space between each, a nailing jig will keep the spacing uniform. Cut a picket the exact width of the opening and attach a cleat to one end. Hang it by the cleat on the rail alongside an at-

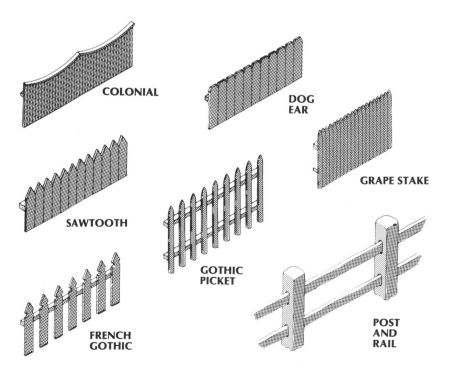

COLONIAL

DOG EAR

GRAPE STAKE

SAWTOOTH

GOTHIC PICKET

FRENCH GOTHIC

POST AND RAIL

PICKET FENCE

tached picket, place the next picket against it, and nail the picket to the rail. Shift the nailing jig to the next space and repeat.

5. Rails can be attached to posts in several ways. If the fence consists only of posts and rails, they can be nailed to the side of the posts or set in mortised slots. If siding is attached to the rails, nail the top rail to the top of the posts and the bottom rail to nailing blocks set at least one foot above ground. Lap the top rails for added strength.

6. To cut pickets, stack the boards four deep, miter them at the desired angle, then turn the stack over and repeat the miter cut. For more intricate patterns, such as gothic or French gothic, stack the boards six deep and cut them on a bandsaw.

7. When making the gate, keep in mind that it requires a diagonal brace running from the top of the frame on the latch side down to the bottom corner on the hinge side. This will keep the frame at the right angles and prevent sagging. Gate width should be at least three feet, and the hinges and latches sturdy and corrosion-resistant.

8. Topping posts are always a good idea, and they also add a nice professional final touch to your fence. Make the topping posts using chamfering and mitering techniques or by turning them on a lathe. Use special fully threaded, no-head screws to secure them to the posts, or make your own dowel pins.

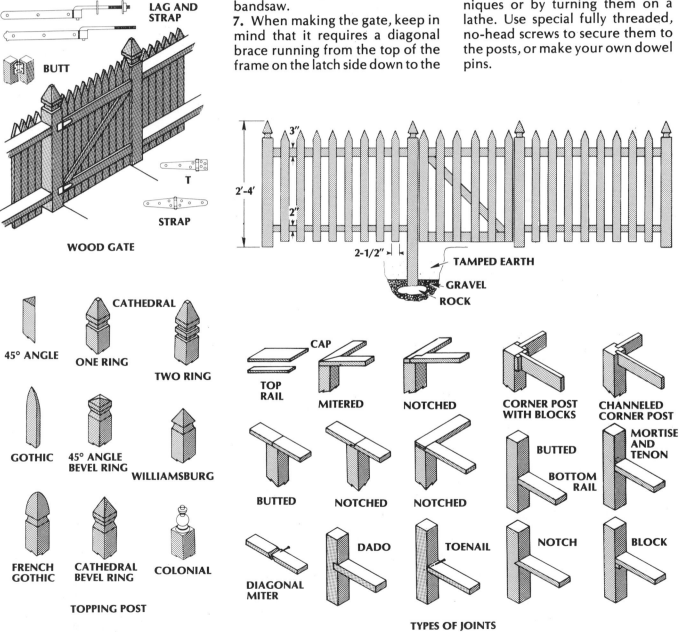

LAG AND STRAP

BUTT

T

STRAP

WOOD GATE

3″

2′-4′

2″

2-1/2″

TAMPED EARTH

GRAVEL

ROCK

45° ANGLE

ONE RING

CATHEDRAL

TWO RING

GOTHIC

45° ANGLE BEVEL RING

WILLIAMSBURG

FRENCH GOTHIC

CATHEDRAL BEVEL RING

COLONIAL

TOPPING POST

CAP

TOP RAIL

MITERED

NOTCHED

CORNER POST WITH BLOCKS

CHANNELED CORNER POST

BUTTED

NOTCHED

NOTCHED

BUTTED

BOTTOM RAIL

MORTISE AND TENON

DIAGONAL MITER

DADO

TOENAIL

NOTCH

BLOCK

TYPES OF JOINTS

LIST OF MATERIALS

(finished dimensions in inches)

A	Legs (4)	1-1/2 × 3-1/2 × 84
B	Leg braces (6)	1-1/2 × 3-1/2 × 27
C	Roof members (13)	3/4 × 3-1/2 × 36
D	Roof supports (2)	1-1/2 × 3-1/2 × 72
E	Upper shelf slats	3/4 × 3-1/2 × 48
F	Upper shelf cross braces (4)	3/4 × 3-1/2 × 12-3/4
G	Middle shelf rails (2)	1-1/2 × 3-1/2 × 72
H	Middle shelf slats (16)	3/4 × 3-1/2 × 24
J	Bottom shelf rails (2)	1-1/2 × 3-1/2 × 48
K	Bottom shelf slats (14)	3/4 × 3-1/2 × 24
	Carriage bolts with wing nuts and washers	1/4 × 3-1/2
	6d Nails	

This unique plant hanger is constructed in sections and fastened with removable bolts and wingnuts so that you can knock it down and take it wherever the light is best.

1. Cut the pieces to size using the dimensions provided.

2. Attach the leg braces (B) to the legs (A) by nailing.

3. Nail the upper shelf cross braces (F) to the legs as shown, then add the upper shelf slats (E).

4. Construct the roof by nailing the roof members (C) to the roof supports (D). The roof members should be spaced approximately 2" apart.

5. Construct the middle shelf module by nailing the middle shelf slats (H) to the middle shelf rails (G). Place three slats at each end of the frame with no space in between; space the middle ten evenly, 1-1/2" apart.

6. Assemble the bottom shelf module by nailing the slats (K) to the bottom shelf rails (J) as was done in the previous step.

7. Join the shelf modules to the legs by drilling 1/4"-diameter bolt holes at the junction of each module; secure with carriage bolts, wing nuts, and washers. Attach the roof by nailing the supports to the legs.

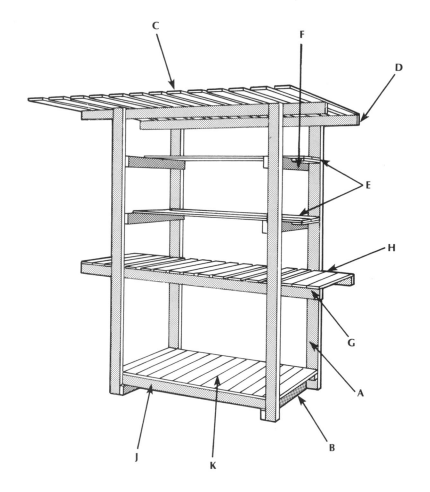

Here's some unique summertime seating that you can put together in less than a weekend. The comfortable reclining seat is made from canvas and fastened with upholstery nails, and the frame is constructed with flathead wood screws and glue.

1. Cut all of the chair parts to length using the dimensions given.

2. Assemble the two front leg pieces (A) and the crosspieces (E) using glue and countersunk screws.

3. Attach the arm pieces (C) to the inside of the front legs using glue and screws. Be sure that all angles are square.

4. Glue and screw the back pieces (D) to the arms; then attach the back leg pieces (B) in the same manner.

5. Level the legs with adjuster blocks (F) as shown.

6. Fill all screwholes with plugs or wood putty, then finish the chair as desired. Be sure to allow sufficient drying time before attaching the seat.

7. Wrap the seat material around the bottom crosspiece as shown, and secure it in back with upholstery nails. You will probably want to add padding to the back where indicated.

LIST OF MATERIALS

(finished dimensions in inches)

A	Front leg pieces (4)	1-1/2 × 1-1/2 × 24
B	Back leg pieces (4)	1-1/2 × 1-1/2 × 22-1/2
C	Arm pieces (4)	1-1/2 × 1-1/2 × 24
D	Back pieces (3)	1-1/2 × 1-1/2 × 23
E	Crosspieces (2)	1-1/2 × 1-1/2 × 23
F	Adjuster blocks (2)	1-1/2 × 1-1/2 × 6
	Brass flathead wood screws	
	Upholstery nails	
	Seat material	24 × 36
	Padding	
	Water-resistant wood glue	

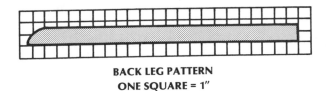

BACK LEG PATTERN
ONE SQUARE = 1"

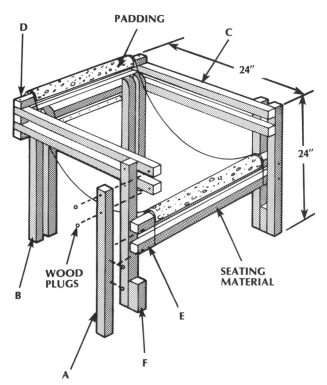

CONSTRUCTION DETAIL

ends to the center board at the top. This completes the table assembly.

6. Begin the bench assembly by nailing benchtop pieces (E) to the bench cleats (F). Leave a 1" gap between the top pieces.

7. Construct the bench legs and attach them to the cleats using the technique described in steps 3 and 4.

8. Cut the bench braces (H) at 45° angles on each end. Use lag bolts to attach the braces to the bottom of the benches and legs.

9. To retain the original color of the redwood, use a semitransparent stain to finish the table and benches. Otherwise, let them weather naturally to a driftwood gray.

This classic picnic table can be the start of many outdoor family gatherings. Despite its generous proportions, the separate benches make it easy to transport. Redwood is recommended because of its natural weathering properties.

1. Cut all of the pieces to size according to the dimensions provided. Cut the bottoms of the table legs (C) at 40° angles, and the bottoms of the bench legs (G) at 20° angles.

2. Begin the table assembly by spacing the tabletop pieces (A) 1/2" apart and nailing them to the table cleats (B).

3. Set the bottoms of the legs against a straightedge, cross them at the middle, then mark and cut lap joints.

4. Bolt the legs together with 1/4" × 2" carriage bolts; attach the legs to the cleats with 1/4" × 3-1/2" carriage bolts.

5. Attach the table braces (D) to the legs with lag bolts and nail the

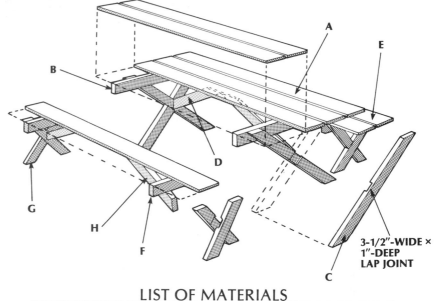

3-1/2"-WIDE × 1"-DEEP LAP JOINT

LIST OF MATERIALS

(finished dimensions in inches)

A	Tabletop pieces (5)	1-1/2 × 5-1/2 × 60
B	Table cleats (2)	1-1/2 × 3-1/2 × 28
C	Table legs (4)	1-1/2 × 3-1/2 × 40
D	Table braces (2)	1-1/2 × 3-1/2 × 30
E	Benchtop pieces (4)	1-1/2 × 5-1/2 × 60
F	Bench cleats (4)	1-1/2 × 3-1/2 × 12
G	Bench legs (8)	1-1/2 × 3-1/2 × 22
H	Bench braces (4)	1-1/2 × 3-1/2 × 15
	10d heavy-duty galvanized nails	
	Lag bolts	1/4 × 3
	Carriage bolts	1/4 × 2
	Carriage bolts	1/4 × 3-1/2
	Nuts and washers	

RECTANGULAR PLANTER BOX

Display your prize plants and flowers in this roomy planter box. It's a snap to build, so why not make one for a friend as well while you're at it?

1. Cut the parts to size according to the dimensions provided.

2. Assemble the top frame, nailing the sides (A) and ends (B) into a rectangle with 5d galvanized nails.

3. Assemble the base frame, nailing the sides (C) and ends (D) into a rectangle with 12d galvanized nails. Nail the bottom pieces (E) in place as shown.

4. Nail the side pieces (F) to the top and base frames. Note that the frames will extend 1-1/2" above and below the sides.

5. Assemble the trim cap by inserting dowels (J) into the sides (G) and ends (H) to form a rectangle; then secure it to the top frame. Finish the planter box as desired.

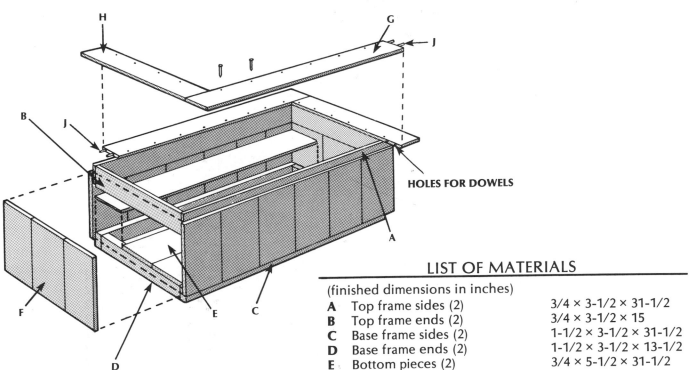

HOLES FOR DOWELS

LIST OF MATERIALS

(finished dimensions in inches)

A	Top frame sides (2)	3/4 × 3-1/2 × 31-1/2
B	Top frame ends (2)	3/4 × 3-1/2 × 15
C	Base frame sides (2)	1-1/2 × 3-1/2 × 31-1/2
D	Base frame ends (2)	1-1/2 × 3-1/2 × 13-1/2
E	Bottom pieces (2)	3/4 × 5-1/2 × 31-1/2
F	Side pieces (18)	3/4 × 5-1/2 × 10
G	Trim cap sides (2)	3/4 × 3-1/2 × 33-1/4
H	Trim cap ends (2)	3/4 × 3-1/2 × 18-1/4
J	Dowels (8)	3 dia. × 3
	5d galvanized finishing nails	
	12d galvanized finishing nails	

This attractive drop-leaf serving cart has many uses, from garden to gazebo and dining room to deck. The casters make it easy to move, and there is ample storage space.

1. Glue up panels for the top (A), shelf (B), and leaves (C) out of 2 × 4 stock. After the panels dry, sand them flat and cut them to the listed dimensions. If the cart will be left outdoors, strengthen the joints between panel strips with dowels or splines and use waterproof glue.

2. Construct the side frames by connecting the stiles (D) and rails (E) with dowels and glue. Cut identical 1-1/2" radius curves on all corners.

3. Round over the upper and lower edges on all four sides of the top, shelf, and leaves using a router and a 1/4"-radius rounding over bit. To minimize splintering, cut across the end grain first, then out along

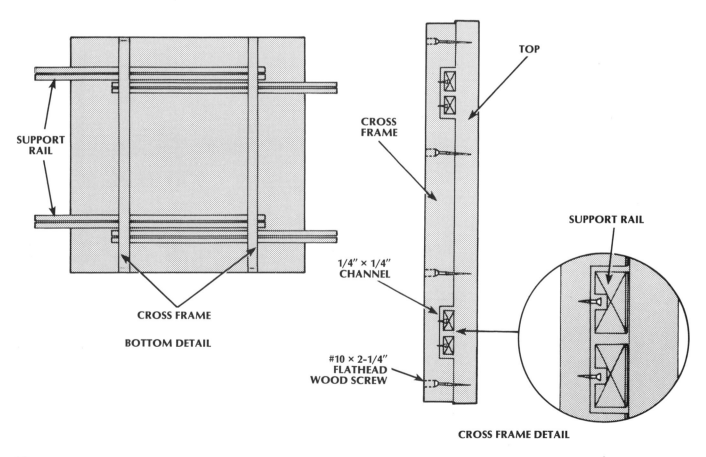

SUPPORT RAIL

CROSS FRAME

BOTTOM DETAIL

TOP

CROSS FRAME

1/4" × 1/4" CHANNEL

#10 × 2-1/4" FLATHEAD WOOD SCREW

SUPPORT RAIL

CROSS FRAME DETAIL

the sides. Also, round over all four edges along the length of the stretchers (F) and the inner and outer edges of the two side frames. Sand off machine marks from the edges before assembling the cart.

4. Dowel and glue the stretchers into the frames, 9" down from the top and 1-3/4" from the outside edge. The stretchers serve as stops when the leaves are in the dropped position.

5. Center the top between the frame rails, spacing the #10 × 2-1/4" flathead wood screws as shown. Counterbore the screws and plug the holes with wood buttons.

6. Position the shelf so that its top surface is flush with the top of the bottom frame rail. Secure with screws and plug.

7. Cut 7/8"-deep × 4"-wide notches in the cross frames (G) as shown. Insert #8 × 2-1/4" flathead wood screws 1" from each side of the notches to serve as stops for the support rails (H). The screws should protrude no more than 3/16".

LIST OF MATERIALS

(finished dimensions in inches)

A	Top	1-1/2 × 23-1/2 × 23-1/2
B	Shelf	1-1/2 × 23-1/2 × 23-1/2
C	Leaves (2)	1-1/2 × 14 × 23-3/8
D	Frame stiles (4)	1-1/2 × 3-1/2 × 28
E	Frame rails (4)	1-1/2 × 3-1/2 × 20
F	Stretchers (2)	1-1/2 × 3-1/2 × 23-1/2
G	Cross frames (2)	3/4 × 1-1/2 × 23-1/2
H	Support rails (4)	3/4 × 1-1/2 × 22
	Brass flathead wood screws	#8 × 2-1/4
	Brass flathead wood screws	#10 × 2-1/4
	Dowels	3/8 dia. × 2
	Wood scraps	1/4 × 1/4 × 1/2
	Butt hinges (4)	
	Casters	
	Wood buttons	
	Water-resistant wood glue	

8. Rout 1/4" × 1/4" channels centered on the bottoms of the support rails.

9. Screw the cross frames to the underside of the top, approximately 6" from the ends. Insert the support rails, and glue a wood scrap in the end of the groove on each rail to prevent the rails from being pulled out when the leaves are opened.

10. Hinge the leaves to the top.

11. Finally, sand and finish, then install the casters.

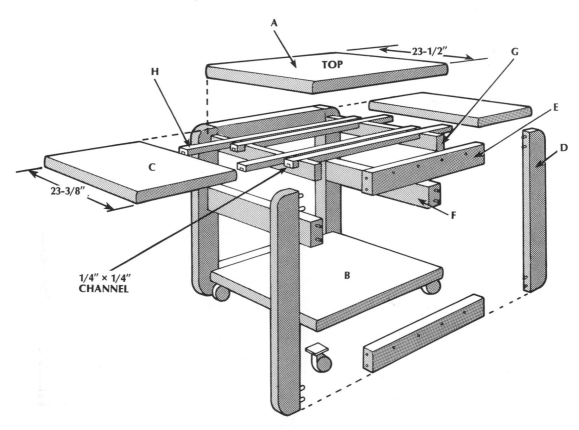

Add some style to your backyard or patio with this attractive deck table. As always, make sure that any parts of the table that contact the ground are made of pressure-treated wood, and use noncorrosive screws and bolts and galvanized nails to avoid staining.

1. Cut the various parts of the table to size (with the exception of the top pieces) using the dimensions provided.

2. Cut pieces for the top (A) from 8- and 12-foot boards and glue them up. When the glue has dried, add the trim (B, C) using finishing nails and glue.

3. Attach the stringers (D) to the underside of the top using #8 × 2" wood screws.

4. Assemble the leg pieces (E, F, G, H) as shown. Nail from both sides, or use 1/4" × 7" carriage bolts.

5. To attach the legs to the top, use 1/4" × 8" carriage bolts. This allows the top to be removed for storing the table.

6. Sand the table and finish as desired.

LIST OF MATERIALS

(finished dimensions in inches)

A	Top	1-1/2 × 49-1/2 × 48
B	Trim (2)	1-1/2 × 1-1/2 × 49-1/2
C	Trim (2)	1-1/2 × 1-1/2 × 51
D	Stringers (2)	1-1/2 × 3-1/2 × 44
E	Legs (8)	1-1/2 × 5-1/2 × 28-1/4
F	Center leg stretchers (4)	1-1/2 × 3-1/2 × 12
G	Bottom leg spacers (4)	1-1/2 × 3-1/2 × 8-1/2
H	Top leg spacers (4)	3-1/2 × 3-1/2 × 5-1/2
	6d galvanized finishing nails	
	Carriage bolts	1/4 × 7
	Carriage bolts	1/4 × 8
	Brass flathead wood screws	#8 × 2
	Water-resistant wood glue	

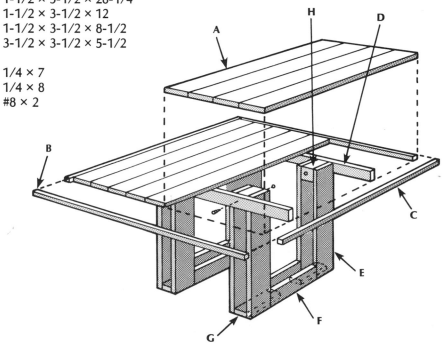

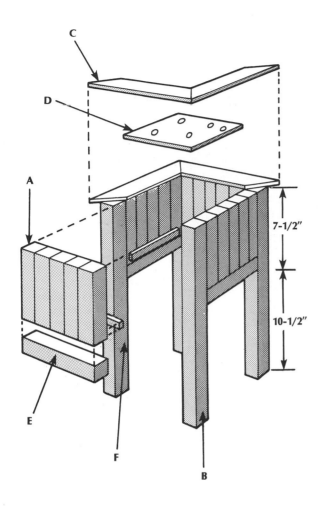

LIST OF MATERIALS

(finished dimensions in inches)

A	Sides (4)	1-1/2 × 7-1/2 × 6
B	Legs (4)	1-1/2 × 1-1/2 × 18
C	Top trim (4)	3/4 × 2-1/2 × 12-1/2
D	Shelf	1/2 × 7-1/2 × 7-1/2 plywood
E	Side supports (4)	1-1/2 × 1-1/2 × 7-1/2
F	Shelf supports (4)	1/2 × 3/4 × 6-1/2
	4d galvanized finishing nails	
	8d galvanized finishing nails	
	Water-resistant wood glue	

You could outfit your home inside and out with this handsome pedestal planter. The legs in this example are 18″ high, but you might want to cut longer or shorter ones, depending on your needs.

1. Cut all of the pieces to size according to the dimensions provided.

2. Lay the side pieces (A) edge to edge in groups of five and glue them up.

3. Nail the legs (B), side supports (E), and shelf supports (F) to the sides as shown.

4. Miter the corners of the top trim (C) and nail them in place as shown.

5. Drill several 1/2″-diameter holes in the shelf (D) for drainage, then set it in place. (The shelf can also be glued in place permanently if desired.)

PET HOUSE

This pet house features a shingle-style roof made of beveled siding. To keep your pet warm and dry during inclement weather, use redwood or pressure-treated wood.

1. Cut all of the pieces to size according to the dimensions given.

2. Construct the floor by nailing the decking (F) to the floor joists (G).

3. Build the frame (A, B, C, D, E) as shown, nailing it directly to the floor.

4. Assemble the roof and back (H) by nailing the individual pieces of siding to the frame, working from bottom to top. Use a 3/4" to 1" overlap as shown to keep out moisture.

5. Add the side wall pieces (J) and front wall pieces (K, L) by nailing and gluing.

6. Assemble the roof cap pieces (M), nail the roof cap in place, and caulk. Finish as desired.

LIST OF MATERIALS

(finished dimensions in inches)

A	Frame, top horizontals (2)	1-1/2 × 1-1/2 × 33
B	Frame, top diagonals (2)	1-1/2 × 1-1/2 × 27
C	Frame, back diagonals (3)	1-1/2 × 1-1/2 × 36
D	Frame, verticals (4)	1-1/2 × 1-1/2 × 25-1/2
E	Frame, bottom horizontals (2)	1-1/2 × 1-1/2 × 32-1/2
F	Decking (4)	3/4 × 11-1/4 × 48
G	Floor joists (3)	1-1/2 × 3-1/2 × 46
H	Roof and back pieces (14)	1/2 × 5-1/2 × 48 beveled siding
J	Side wall pieces (18)	3/8 × 5-1/2 × varying lengths
K	Front wall pieces (2)	3/8 × 5-1/2 × 36
L	Front wall pieces (10)	3/8 × 5-1/2 × 12
M	Roof cap pieces (2)	3/4 × 2-1/2 × 48
	4d galvanized nails	
	7d galvanized nails	
	Caulk	
	Water-resistant wood glue	

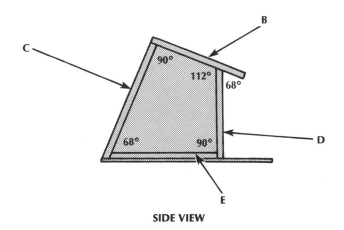

SIDE VIEW

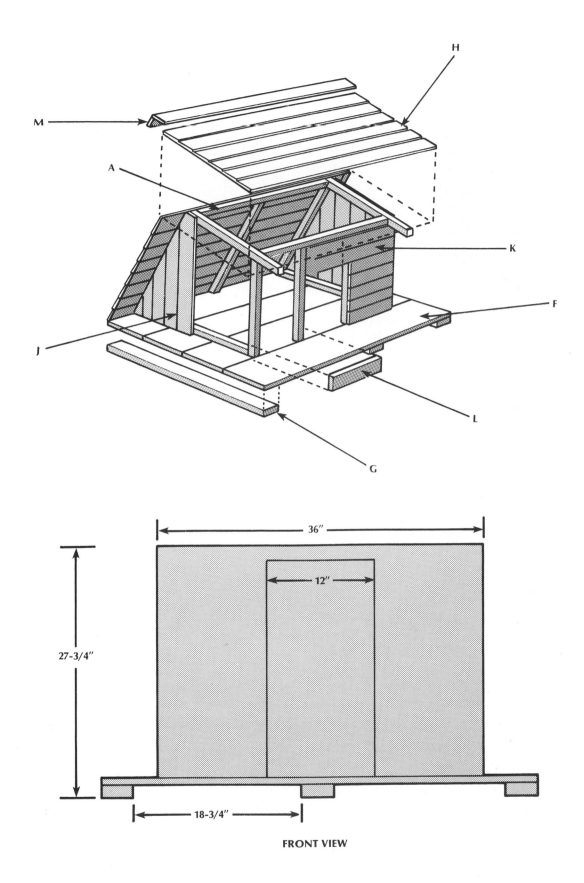

FRONT VIEW

You don't even need a deck to enjoy the comforts of this knockdown deck chair. And when it's not in use, just take it apart and store it away.

1. Cut all parts to size. Use the patterns provided to make templates for the back legs (A), seat legs (B), and top slat (E).

2. Use a saber saw or keyhole saw to cut out the handle opening in the top slat.

3. Round the corners and edges of all slats and legs; then sand.

4. Drill 1/2"-diameter counterbore plug holes for screws 1-5/8" in from the ends on the top slat and back slats (C), 3-1/4" in from the ends on the seat slats (D), and 3/4" in from the ends on the support slats (F).

5. Locate the lower support slat on the face of the back legs 11" up from the bottom, then screw it in place. There should be 14-1/2" between the inside of the legs.

6. Locate the upper support slat on the back of the back legs, leaving 3-3/4" between the slats.

7. Locate and screw the back slats in place, beginning with the top slat and working down. Leave 1/2" between slats.

8. Locate and screw the seat slats in place, beginning with the outermost slat. Leave 1/2" between slats and 14-3/8" between the outside of the legs.

9. Test for fit of the sections; if any pieces bind, they can be adjusted by sanding.

10. Install the plugs, allow the glue to dry thoroughly, then sand. Finish as desired.

11. Slide the seat legs through the support slats. The chair is ready to use.

LIST OF MATERIALS

(finished dimensions in inches)

A	Back legs (2)	1-1/2 × 5-1/2 × 40
B	Seat legs (2)	1-1/2 × 5-1/2 × 36
C	Back slats (6)	3/4 × 1-1/2 × 20
D	Seat slats (8)	3/4 × 1-1/2 × 20
E	Top slat	3/4 × 3-1/2 × 20
F	Support slats (2)	3/4 × 1-1/2 × 17-1/2
	Brass flathead wood screws	#8 × 2
	Plugs	
	Water-resistant wood glue	

ONE SQUARE = 1"

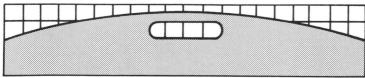

TOP SLAT

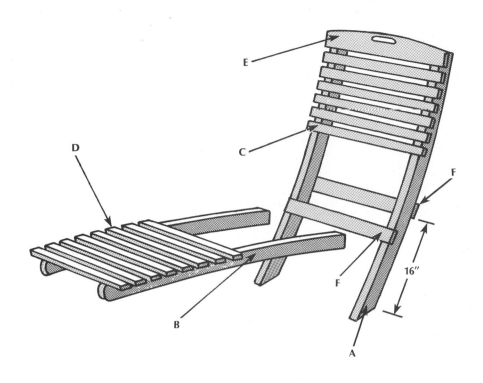

E

D

C

F

B

F

16"

A

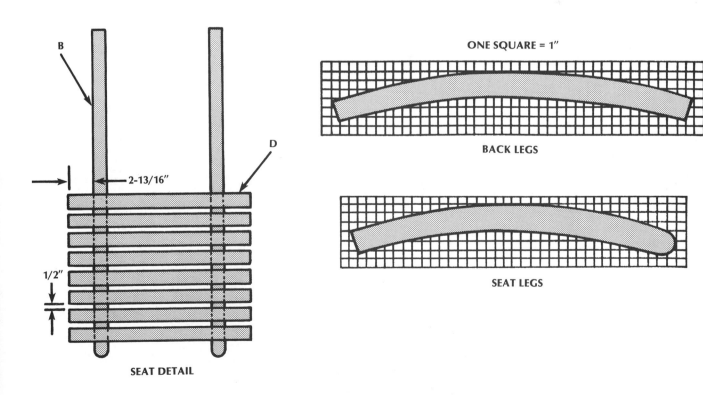

B

D

2-13/16"

1/2"

SEAT DETAIL

ONE SQUARE = 1"

BACK LEGS

SEAT LEGS

SLAT-TOPPED BENCH

This is also known as a "duckboard" bench because the gaps between the slats let water drain right through. Indoors or out, it's a practical addition to any home.

1. Cut all of the pieces to size according to the dimensions provided.

2. Cut identical curves on both ends of the slats (A) and on the bottoms of the legs (E).

3. Cut a 3/4"-deep × 1-1/2"-wide rabbet in the tops of the legs.

4. Attach the end rails (D) to the legs as shown with dowels and glue. The top rails should be level with the bottoms of the rabbets and with the bottom rails 8" below. Attach the side rails (C) in the same manner. Double-check to make sure the assembly is square.

5. Assemble the top by screwing and gluing together six of the eight slats, alternating them with spacers (B) as shown. Locate the spacers 3" from the ends of the slats, with the assembly flush on the underside.

6. Set the top within the legs of the base assembly. Attach the two remaining slats to the rabbets, counterboring and plugging the holes.

7. Sand the entire bench and finish as desired.

LIST OF MATERIALS

(finished dimensions in inches)

A	Slats (8)	1-1/2 × 3-1/2 × 48
B	Spacers (10)	3/4 × 1-1/2 × 3-1/2
C	Side rails (2)	1-1/2 × 1-1/2 × 35
D	End rails (4)	1-1/2 × 1-1/2 × 12-3/4
E	Legs (4)	1-1/2 × 3-1/2 × 16-3/4
	Brass flathead wood screws	#8 × 2
	Dowels	5/8 dia × 2-1/2
	Water-resistant wood glue	

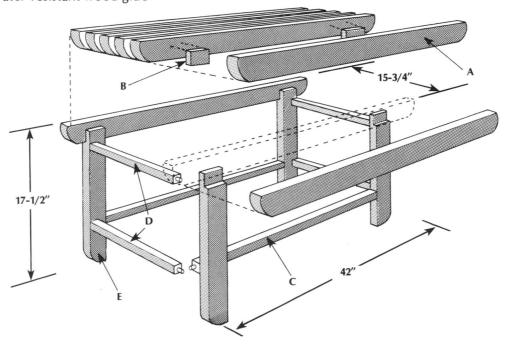

Take this spacious sandbox, add a wading pool and a beach umbrella, and you have a beach for the children right in your own backyard. The storage bins are perfect for keeping pails, shovels, and other playthings. Because this sandbox has no bottom, it should be lined with black plastic before being filled to prevent weeds from growing up through the sand. Be sure to include holes in the plastic for drainage.

1. After cutting all of the pieces to size, mark and drill holes in the ends (A) to accommodate lag bolts.

2. Attach supports (D) flush to the bottom edges of the ends.

3. Assemble the sandbox as shown, using lag bolts and washers to connect the ends and sides (B).

4. Set the bottoms (C) in place and secure with screws. It is a good idea to drill a few holes in the bottoms for drainage, especially if you live in a wet climate.

5. Assemble the storage lids (E) by screwing the braces (F) from underneath as shown. Attach with hinges.

6. After finishing, make lid supports using eye screws and rope. As an alternative, you might want to use special hardware to prevent children from dropping the lids on their fingers.

LIST OF MATERIALS

(finished dimensions in inches)

A	Ends (2)	1-1/2 × 11-1/4 × 96
B	Sides (4)	1-1/2 × 11-1/4 × 92-1/2
C	Storage bottoms (2)	1-1/2 × 11-1/4 × 92-1/2
D	Supports (4)	1-1/2 × 1-1/2 × 92-1/2
E	Storage lids (4)	1-1/2 × 14-1/2 × 48
F	Storage lid braces (12)	1-1/2 × 1-1/2 × 10-1/4
	Brass flathead wood screws	#6 × 2
	Lag bolts and washers	5/16 × 3-1/2
	Eye screws	
	Hinges	
	Rope	
	Masonry sand	

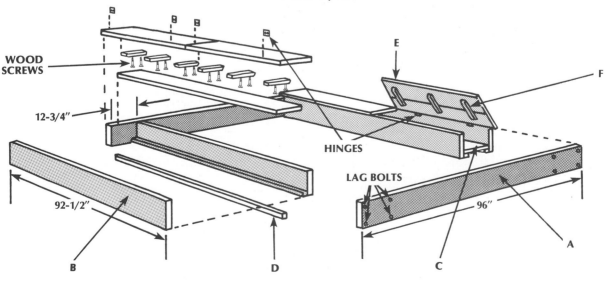

WOOD SCREWS

12-3/4"

92-1/2"

HINGES

LAG BOLTS

E

F

96"

A

B

D

C

Index

CREDITS

American Plywood Assn. (1119 A Street, Tacoma, Washington, 98401): Early American Wall Shelf.

Georgia-Pacific Corp. (133 Peachtree Street NE, Atlanta, Georgia, 30307): Stacking Boxes.

Louisiana-Pacific Corp. (111 SW Fifth Avenue, Portland, Oregon, 97205): Desk/Workbench.

Rodale Press, Inc. (33 E. Minor Street, Emmaus, Pennsylvania, 18098): Children's Furniture.

Shopsmith®, Inc. (3931 Image Drive, Dayton, Ohio, 45414): Cassette Case; Relish Tray; Deer Bookends and Candleholders; Wine Server; Round Picture Frame; Serving Tray; Candle Sconce; Wooden Jewelry; Lantern; Mirror with Planter; Napkin Holder; Shelf Brackets; Candlesticks; Hurricane Lamp; Puzzles; Cedar Ornaments; Log Cradle; Hanging Double Planter; Wine Bottle Rack; Gym/Play Center; Sandbox; Patio Cart; Picnic Table/ Bench; Redwood Planter; Lawn Chair; Wood Fence; Lawn Table.

The Know Place. (4038-128 Avenue SE, Suite 176, Bellevue, Washington, 98009): Garden or Entryway Lamp; Wind Chimes; Divider Screen; Mirrored Coffee Table; Table and Bench; Planter Box; Birdhouse; Plant Hanger; Deck Chair; Rectangular Picnic Table; Rectangular Planter Box; Serving Cart; Deck Table; Pedestal Planter; Pet House; Knockdown Deck Chair; Slat-Topped Bench; Sandbox with Storage.

The Book Club offers a wood identification kit that includes 30 samples of cabinet woods. For details on ordering, please write: Book Club, Member Services, P.O. Box 2033, Latham, N.Y. 12111.